*Law*Basics

SUCCESSION

AUSTRALIA
LBC Information Services
Sydney

CANADA and USA
Carswell
Toronto

NEW ZEALAND
Brooker's
Auckland

SINGAPORE and MALAYSIA
Sweet & Maxwell Asia
Singapore and Kuala Lumpur

*Law*Basics

SUCCESSION

Second edition

By

Alasdair Bothwell Gordon,
B.D. (Hons), LL.B., Ed.D, T.Q.F.E., L.C.G.I.
Formerly Lecturer in Law, Aberdeen College

THOMSON

™

W. GREEN

First published 1999

Published in 2007 by W. Green & Son Limited
21 Alva Street
Edinburgh EH2 4PS

Typeset by LBJ Typesetting Ltd, Kingsclere

Printed in Great Britain by Athenaeum Press,
Gateshead, Tyne & Wear

No natural forests were destroyed to make this product;
only farmed timber was used and replanted.

A CIP catalogue record of this book is available from the British
Library.

ISBN 978-0-414-01682-8

© W. Green and Son Limited
2007

CONTENTS

Page

Table of Cases vii

1. Introduction to Succession 1
2. Survivorship 7
3. Legal Rights 11
4. Intestate Succession 17
5. Essential and Formal Validity 29
6. Common Testamentary Provisions 40
7. Residuary and Substitutionary Provisions 50
8. Vesting and Accretion 53
9. Alterations and Additions 62
10. Will Substitutes. 67
11. Interpretation of Wills 74
12. The Executor's Role and Duties 79
13. Trusts 96

Appendix 1: Sample Examination Questions and Answer
             Plans 108
Appendix 2: A Typical Trust Disposition and Settlement. ... 116

Index 121

TABLE OF CASES

ABERDEEN RY CO v Blaikie Bros (1853) 1 Macq. 461 101
Aitken's Trs v Aitken, 1927 S.C. 374 41
Anderson v Smoke (1898) 25 R. 493 76
Andrews v Ewart's Trs (1886) 13 R. (H.L.) 69 99
Angus' Exrx v Batchan's Trs, 1949 S.C. 335 76
Arres' Trs v Mather (1881) 9 R. 107 62
Ayrshire Hospice, Petrs, 1993 S.L.T. (Sh. Ct) 75, Sh Ct (South Strathclyde) 37

BARCLAY'S EXR v McLeod (1880) 7 R. 477 77
Barclay's Trs v Watson (1903) 5 F. 926 73
Barclays Bank Ltd v McGreish, 1983 S.L.T. 344, OH 70
Bisset v Walker, 26 Nov. 1799, Fac Coll. 71
Braithwaite v Bank of Scotland, 1999 S.L.T. 25; 1997 G.W.D. 40—2037,
    OH 33
Bruce's J.F. v Lord Advocate, 1969 S.C. 296; 1969 S.L.T. 337, IH (2 Div) . . 65, 66
Burgess' Trs v Crawford, 1912 S.C. 387 99

CAITHNESS (EARL OF) v Sinclair, 1912 S.C. 79 41
Carmichael's Exrs v Carmichael, 1909 S.C. 1387 35
Cathcart's Trs v Allardice (1899) 2 F. 326 50
Cathcart's Trs v Bruce, 1923 S.L.T. 722 75
Cherry's Trs v Patrick, 1911 S.L.T. 313 101
Chisholm v Chisholm, 1949 S.C. 434 34
Christie's Exrx v Armstrong, 1996 S.C. 295; 1996 S.L.T. 948, IH (2 Div) 69
Clark v Clark's Exrx, 1989 S.C. 84; 1989 S.L.T. 665, OH 101
Clarke v Carfin Coal Co. (1891) 18 R. (H.L.) 63 14
Clyde v Clyde, 1958 S.C. 343; 1958 S.L.T. 256, OH 64
Coats' Trs v Coats, 1914 S.C. 744 15
Colville, Petr, 1962 S.C. 185; 1962 S.L.T. 45, IH (1 Div) 98
Couper's J.F. v Valentine; sub nom McGill v Valentine, 1976 S.C. 63; 1976
    S.L.T. 83, OH 78
Cross, Petr, 1987 S.L.T. 384; 1987 S.C.L.R. 356, OH 95
Crumpton's J.F. v Barnardo's Homes, 1917 S.C. 713 . . . . 53, 116
Cullen's Exr v Elphinstone, 1948 S.C. 662 65

DINWOODIE'S EXRX v Carruther's Exr (1895) 23 R. 234 71
Douglas-Hamilton v Duke and Duchess of Hamilton's Trs, 1961 S.C. 205;
    1961 S.L.T. 305, IH (1 Div) 50
Dow v Kilgour's Trs (1877) 4 R. 403 42
Draper v Thomson, 1954 S.C. 136 34
Dundee Mags v Morris (1858) 3 Macq. 134 76
Duthie's Exrs v Taylor, 1986 S.L.T. 142, OH 65

ELDER'S TRS v Free Church of Scotland (1892) 20 R. 2 .... 43, 112

FLEMING'S TRS v Fleming; sub nom Jackson v Fleming, 2000 S.C. 206; 2000
S.L.T. 406, IH (Ex Div) 71
Fortnato's J.F. v Fortunato, 1981 S.L.T. 277, OH 75
Fraser v Rose (1849) 11 D. 1466 41
Fraser's Trs v Fraser, 1980 S.L.T. 211, OH 61

GARDNER'S EXRS v Raeburn, 1996 S.L.T. 745; 1995 S.C.L.R. 864, OH 70
Gilchrist, Petr, 1990 S.L.T. 494, OH 95
Gilles v Glasgow Royal Infirmary, 1960 S.C. 438 62
Greig v Merchant Company of Edinburgh, 1921 S.C. 76 8

HONEYMAN'S EXR v Sharp; sub nom Rodgers v Sharp, 1978 S.C. 223; 1979
S.L.T. 177, OH 32
Hunter's Exrs, Petrs, 1992 S.C. 474; 1992 S.L.T. 1141, IH (2 Div) 95

JOHNSTON v Dobie (1783) Mor.5443 3
Johnson's Will Trusts, Re [1967] Ch. 387; [1967] 2 W.L.R. 152; [1967] 1 All
E.R. 553, Ch D 41

KEILLER v Thomson's Trs (1826) 4 S. 724 75
Kerr, Petr, 1968 S.L.T. (Sh. Ct) 61 23
Knox v Mackinnon (1888) 15 R. (H.L.) 83 104

LINDSAY'S TRS v Lindsay, 1931 S.C. 586 44

MCBEATH'S TRS v McBeath, 1935 S.C. 471 34
McCaig v University of Glasgow, 1907 S.C. 231 41
McCaig's Trs v Lismore United Free Kirk Session, 1915 S.C. 426 41
Macdonald v Cuthbertson (1890) 18 R. 101 35
Mackintosh's J.F. v Lord Advocate, 1935 S.C. 406 41
Miller's Trs v Miller (1890) 18 R. 301 .... 42, 107
Milne v Smith, 1982 S.L.T. 129, OH 77
Mitchell's Administratrix v Edinburgh Royal Infirmary, 1928 S.C. 47 66
Morgan Guaranty Trust Co of New York v Lothian RC, 1995 S.C. 151;
1995 S.L.T. 299, IH (Ct of 5 judges) 106
Morrison v Maclean's Trs (1862) 24 D. 625 31
Muir v City of Glasgow Bank (1879) 6 R. (H.L.) 21 104
Munro v Coutts (1813) 1 Dow 437 37

NAISMYTH v Boyes (1899) 1 F. (H.L.) 79 11
Nisbet's Trs v Nisbet (1871) 9 M. 937 31

OBERS v Paton's Trs (1897) 24 R. 719 16

PAXTON'S TRS v Cowie (1886) 13 R. 1191 60

REDFERN'S EXRS v Redfern, 1996 S.L.T. 900, OH 70
Reid's Trs v Dawson, 1915 S.C. (H.L.) 47 77

Rhodes v Peterson, 1971 S.C. 56; 1972 S.L.T. 98, OH 34, 37
Robbie's J.F. v Macrae (1893) 20 R. 358 76
Robert's Trs v Roberts (1903) 5 F. 541 61
Robertson's J.F. v Robertson, 1968 S.L.T. 32; 1967 S.L.T. (Notes) 113, OH 77
Ross's J.F v Martin, 1955 S.C. (H.L.) 56 9
Russo v Russo, 1998 S.L.T. (Sh. Ct) 32 28

SALVESEN'S TRS v Wye, 1954 S.C. 440 99
Secretary of State for Scotland v Sutherland, 1944 S.C. 79 7
Smith, Petr, 1979 S.L.T. (Sh. Ct) 35 94
Sprot's Trs v Sprot, 1909 S.C. 272 37
Stewart v Stewart (1891) 19 R. 310 93
Sutherland's Tr. v Verschoyle, 1968 S.L.T. 43; 1967 S.L.T. (Notes) 106, IH
   (2 Div) 42

THELLUSON v Woodford (1799) 4 Ves. 227; (1805) 11 Ves. 112 .... 42, 112
Thomson's Trs v Bowhill Baptist Church, 1956 S.L.T. 302 65
Thomson's Trs v Davidson, 1947 S.C. 654 102

WATSON v Giffen (1884) 11 R. 444 .... 53, 116
Wedderspoon v Thomson's Trs (1824) 3 S. 396 75
Williamson v Williamson, 1997 S.C. 94; 1997 S.L.T. 1044, IH (Ex Div) 33, 35
Wright's Trs v Callender, 1993 S.C. (H.L.) 13; 1993 S.L.T. 556, HL 78

YULE'S TRS, 1981 S.L.T. 250, IH (1 Div) 74

1. INTRODUCTION TO SUCCESSION

PRELIMINARY COMMENTS

The first edition of this book appeared in 1999. Subsequent legislation has made a new edition not only desirable but necessary.

The major changes have come about firstly by the enactment of the Civil Partnership Act 2004 (the "2004 Act"). This is a piece of UK legislation, enacted in Westminster with the consent of the Scottish Parliament. Chapter 3 of this substantial Act deals exclusively with Scotland. Put simply, the Act permits individuals of the same sex to enter into a civil partnership, the effects and consequences of which are broadly similar to marriage. This means that a surviving civil partner has similar rights of succession as a surviving husband or wife.

This book does not deal in detail with the provisions of the 2004 Act, apart from the changes in the law of succession. The writer found himself in somewhat of a quandary as to the most appropriate way of describing a "spouse or civil partner". It was tempting to opt for the shorthand "partner". However, that might cause confusion. In popular speech, the word "partner" can mean spouse, civil partner or cohabitee. Accordingly, the reader may assume that, throughout this book, "spouse" generally includes a civil partner but excludes a cohabitee.

The second major set of changes has come about through the Family Law (Scotland) Act 2006 (the "2006 Act"). This Act introduces important new and groundbreaking rights to cohabiting couples; these rights, however, are not identical to those of spouses or civil partners. The 2006 Act also finally phases out the last vestiges of irregular marriage in Scotland, subject to certain exceptions.

The third series of changes are found in the Charities and Trustee Investment (Scotland) Act 2005, where that statute affects the investment powers of all trustees.

Finally, the Human Tissue (Scotland) Act 2006 makes provision for regularising the use of body parts for transplantation or research.

This raft of new legislation has yet to be interpreted by case law.

HISTORICAL BACKGROUND

Succession, that area of law which regulates the rights of survivors over the property of a deceased person, may be traced back to the most ancient legal systems. It deals mainly with two elements, property and persons. To put it another way, among the questions which will arise on the occurrence of most deaths are "What property is there?" and "Who gets what?". In all civilised legal systems, the law has had to maintain an uneasy balance between putting the wishes of the deceased into effect and treating the survivors, particularly close members of the family, in a fair and equitable manner.

In the Old Testament (Genesis 15,2), it can be seen that, if Abraham had not had a son, his heir would have been the son of his slave. In that ancient situation, succession was concerned with the continuation of the family line at least as much as the passing on of property. Modern succession looks much more at the property element. In the ancient world, where normally succession favoured the first born and male, the commonest reason for adoption was to provide for succession. Curiously enough, in Scots law, it is only in comparatively recent times that an adopted child has had any rights to succeed to the estate of an adoptive parent. Even now, an adopted child cannot inherit a title or coat of arms from an adoptive parent.

Though we bring nothing into this world and take nothing out of it, people accumulate rights in property during their lives. Even the poorest person normally leaves something, even if only the clothes he stands up in. Some people leave vast amounts of property; the majority leave more modest amounts. Whether the amounts left are large or small, the basic law of succession is the same. Its principles apply to rich and poor alike.

Succession is an area that can potentially be very divisive among members of a family. Perceptions of what is, or is not, "fair" can be very clouded when it comes to matters of inheritance. Looking at it from another viewpoint, it is natural for older people to think in terms of who will succeed to their property. Very few would want their property to be divided according to rules over which they have no control. Yet it is still only a minority—although an increasing minority—who leave any precise instructions by will as to the disposal of their estate.

HERITABLE AND MOVEABLE PROPERTY

One particular aspect of the law of property which affects succession is the distinction between heritable and moveable property.

This distinction is still important, although less so than it was, prior to the passing of the Succession (Scotland) Act 1964. Before the 1964 Act, part of the law of intestate succession was of feudal origin. The heritable property, or "heritage", passed with a preference in favour of first-born male descendants (the "heir-at-law", in the case of the eldest son) but the surviving spouse enjoyed a liferent of part of the deceased's heritable property named "terce" in the case of a widow and "courtesy" in the case of a widower. Both under pre- and post- 1964 law, a spouse (or civil partner) and children have legal rights against the deceased's *moveable* property. Legal rights will be considered in Chapter 3.

In essence, the distinction between heritable and moveable is simple. Heritable property refers to land and to items permanently attached to it, such as buildings, houses, walls and trees growing in the ground. All property that is not heritable is counted as moveable. Property law also distinguishes between corporeal and incorporeal items, which can be either heritable or moveable. If property is corporeal it has a physical existence and the five senses can, at least in theory, be applied to it. Corporeal property could include land, houses, cars and furnishings. Incorporeal property is invisible and could include items such as a lease, shares in a company and a very wide variety of rights. The distinction between corporeal and incorporeal property has little direct relevance to the law of succession.

In the majority of cases, it is easy to know into which category any given property falls. Most property is obviously either heritable or moveable by nature. There can occasionally be problems. There is, in the law of succession, a particular legal fiction that allows certain moveable property to be "constructively" converted into heritage. Thus, money required for the completion of an unfinished building counts as heritage and heirs would not be able to claim legal rights out of it. In the old case of *Johnston v Dobie* (1783) Mor. 5443, it was held that building materials piled on the ground beside an incomplete structure counted as heritable property.

A particular problem can arise in the case of goodwill of a business. Goodwill is an elusive concept at the best of times, yet anyone buying or selling a business is well aware that it can be a valuable asset. In fact, goodwill may be heritable or moveable or a mixture of the two. If the business is closely associated with particular premises, such as a well known and established hotel, the goodwill will generally count as heritable. If the reputation of the business relied mainly on the deceased's skill and personal reputation, the goodwill will be moveable. Obviously, there are times where the goodwill will be a mixture of the two and a precise apportionment between heritable and moveable may well be problematic.

Another potential problem area is that of fixtures, i.e. items that were moveable but have become part of the heritage. Suppose John buys an Adam mantelpiece and has it built into his living room. At the same time, he has a new fitted carpet laid. He dies, leaving a will providing that his house, i.e. heritage, goes to Robert and the contents, i.e. moveables, to Freda. How does one categorise the Adam mantelpiece and the fitted carpet? Unless the will expressly deals with the matter, the presumptions of the so-called law of fixtures apply. The presumption would be that the mantelpiece is permanently attached to the property and the courts have tended to favour the person entitled to succeed to the heritage, so that he takes it in the same condition in which the deceased enjoyed it. However, the fitted carpet would not count as a permanent attachment and would be a moveable asset.

If the deceased had agreed to sell heritable property but, at the time of death, the transaction had not been settled, the heritage would count as a heritable asset with a nil value but the amount of the price unpaid would be a moveable asset, as would any sum already paid to account. If the deceased had, conversely, agreed to buy heritable property but had not paid for it, that property would count as a heritable asset and the unpaid price would be a moveable debt.

If the deceased's heritable property was mortgaged, i.e. subject to a standard security, the debt, or loan outstanding, counts as heritable and is deducted from the value of the heritage. If the deceased was a creditor in a standard security over another person's property, the value of the security counts as moveable but not in respect of legal rights or taxation, where it counts as heritable (this simply means that legal rights cannot be claimed out of the value of the standard security). The word "mortgage" is used popularly to describe a loan advanced to a buyer of heritable property. Throughout this book, the writer will adhere to this handy, if inaccurate, convention.

Many people who have received a loan secured over their property will have some form of mortgage protection policy to pay off the outstanding capital sum in the event of death. It is important to notice that the secured loan is a heritable debt and the proceeds of the policy count as a moveable asset. The debt is not automatically extinguished.

If the loan is an endowment mortgage, the debtor pays interest only but, in addition, pays premiums on an endowment insurance policy which, at the end of its term or on the earlier death of the insured, will produce (in theory!) at least an adequate sum to repay the original amount borrowed. In a traditional endowment mortgage, the debt is doubly secured. There will be a standard security over the heritable property and the insurance policy will have been assigned to the lender and that assignation duly intimated to the insurance company. In such a case, the debt would be deducted from heritable and moveable estate in proportion to the respective values of the heritage and the policy. If the policy has not been properly assigned to the lender, the debt is not doubly secured and all the proceeds simply count as a moveable asset.

Under section 22 of the Partnership Act 1890, a partner's share in a firm's assets count as moveable, even if some or all of these assets are actually heritable, such as a farming partnership.

A TESTATOR'S RIGHTS

It is a basic rule of property law that we can do what we wish with our own property, subject to only minimal constraints. This is true in succession, but the fact remains that any person, male or female, who has a spouse or civil partner and/or children cannot completely disinherit his/her family. This is due to possible claims for legal rights against the moveable estate, mentioned above and considered in more detail in Chapter 3. Before passing on, it is worth noticing three basic points:

(1) Rights of succession or legacies rank second to debts due by the deceased. To put this another way, the deceased's debts must be paid before his estate can be divided among the beneficiaries. How debts are dealt with is considered further in Chapter 12. It will be demonstrated that the distinction between heritable and moveable is also important in matters of debts against the estate.

(2) A deceased person will be either testate or intestate. If he has left a valid will, he is clearly testate. If he made no will, or left an invalid will, he is said to be intestate. In some cases, a deceased may only have made testamentary provision for some of his property in which case there will be a partial intestacy. Legal rights of a spouse, civil partner and/or children can be claimed against a testate or an intestate estate.

(3) Succession only operates when someone has died. This may sound obvious in the extreme, but it is an important issue that will be further considered in Chapter 2. It follows logically that there also have to be parties who can accept the succession.

MALE AND FEMALE

The modern law of succession does not favour one gender as against another, whatever might have been the case in former times; nor does it favour elder against younger. In the interests of word economy, parties are generally designed as masculine throughout this book, but this is intended to be inclusive. Unless the context clearly indicates otherwise, everything stated in the book should be taken to apply equally to both genders.

INHERITANCE TAX

It has been said that there are only two certainties in life—death and taxes. True or false, the two can be connected. Since the 17th century, successive governments have realised that death can be a convenient time to tax a person's estate. Originally, death duty would be calculated on what the deceased owned at the time of death. An obvious form of avoidance would be for an older person to pass on at least some of his property to his heirs before death. The tax was extended to include property thus transferred for a limited period before death. For most of the 20th century, the main death tax was estate duty, replaced briefly by capital transfer tax. In 1986, this was replaced by inheritance tax ("IHT").

IHT, like most taxation, is complex and continually liable to change. Accordingly, only very general comments can be made in a book of this size and, even then, with the *caveat* that governments can—and do—change their minds.

The IHT Act 1984 provides that IHT is charged on the loss of value caused to an estate when a transfer (death counts as a transfer of the entire estate) is made, unless it is an exempt transfer. If a transfer is made more than seven years before death, it is exempt and no IHT is paid on that property. Thus if A gives his son B £100,000 and dies ten years thereafter, no tax is payable on that sum. But if he dies one year after making the transfer, the result is different. Even when a transfer is made within the seven year period, IHT may be reduced by taper relief depending on when, within that period, the gift was made. Transfers between spouses or civil partners during lifetime or as a result of succession are totally exempt from IHT. Other major exemptions are donations to registered UK charities, political parties or national museums. There are other smaller exemptions for certain gifts and reasonable maintenance of relatives.

The basis of valuation of estates is outlined in Chapter 12 and IHT is charged on the value of the net estate, i.e. after deduction of allowable debts and funeral expenses. At the time of writing, the first £285,000 of an estate is exempt (or, more precisely, is taxed at a nil rate) and thereafter the rate is 40 per cent. Thus, if a total net estate is £300,000, only £15,000 is liable to be taxed at 40 per cent, so the amount charged would be £6,000.

Roughly 20 per cent of all estates are actually liable to IHT. However, any testator whose estate might potentially attract an IHT liability should consider obtaining professional advice.

---

2. SURVIVORSHIP

THE FACT OF DEATH

In the vast majority of cases, the fact as well as the date and time of a person's death can be determined without difficulty. Modern science and medicine have, in some ways, made the concept of death less precise than in the time of our forefathers. Scots law, like most legal systems, is still coming to terms with the distinction between physical death and brain death.

An increasing number of people have what is misleadingly called a living will. This is a basic statement of how the person might wish to be treated in the event of life threatening illness or trauma, e.g. would he wish to be resuscitated? This is a complex area of law, beyond the scope of this book, although some reference is made to it in Chapter 12. It is sufficient at this stage to state that "living will" is a contradiction in terms as it is not a testamentary provision.

Before an estate can be wound up, the date and place of death must be stated and would have to be proved in the rare event of a challenge. An extract from the Register of Deaths is regarded as sufficient (but not conclusive) evidence of death under section 41(3) of the Registration of Births, Marriages and Deaths (Scotland) Act 1965. However, a doctor can only issue a death certificate after viewing identified human remains. Problems obviously arise where there are no such remains.

Under Scottish common law, if a person disappeared, there was no presumption other than that his life continued to the extremes of old age. In *Secretary of State for Scotland v Sutherland*, 1944 S.C. 79, a husband had disappeared and had not been heard of for 42 years. The wife applied for a declarator that he was now dead. The court adhered to the presumption that he was still alive, now aged 72. The length of time presumably showed how successful he had been in avoiding his wife! Anyone trying to overturn the common law presumption also required proof beyond reasonable doubt, a much higher standard than normally required in a civil case. In the earlier case of *Greig v Merchant Company of Edinburgh*, 1921 S.C. 76, a husband had been absent for 10 years. There was good medical evidence that his alcoholic lifestyle would have killed him before then. The court accepted that he was dead and his widow was thus able to claim her pension.

Clearly, the common law was inflexible in this area and could cause considerable distress. There are now statutory presumptions, currently contained in the Presumption of Death (Scotland) Act 1977 (the "1977 Act"). Under this Act, anyone having an interest to do so may raise an action to have a person declared legally dead. This applies in two main circumstances:

(1) It may be that someone is thought to have died at or around a particular time. An obvious example would be where an air accident occurred over the ocean and no human remains could be recovered.

(2) Someone may not have been known to be alive for a period of at least seven years. To put it another way, the person simply disappears. With modern forms of communication and computer databases, it is much more difficult for a living person to disappear, but it is still possible.

Proof of death under the 1977 Act is on a balance of probabilities, as would be normal in civil cases. If it cannot be proved exactly when death took place, but that it must have been between time A and time B, time B will be the date on the court decree. If the deceased has simply disappeared, death will be deemed to have taken place at the end of the day seven years after he was last known to be alive.

The decree allows the executor to proceed with the winding up of the estate. Insurance companies need not allow payment of a life policy proceeds purely on the evidence of a declarator of death although, in practice, most do. The missing person's marriage is dissolved once for all and that includes any related right to social security benefits. Thus, if the deceased were to reappear, like Robinson Crusoe, his marriage would not be revived—although any criminal liability would. If he did reappear, obviously it would be necessary for him to apply for a recall of the declarator of death. Such applications are rare but not unknown.

SURVIVORSHIP

Regrettably, common calamities where more than one person is killed in the same incident occur quite regularly. An easy example is a car crash. The basic rule of succession is that rights pass on to, or "vest" (see Chapter 8), only in those who survive the deceased. In normal circumstances, it is not difficult to prove who survived whom, but it may be extremely difficult in the case of a common calamity where two people are killed around the same time. If, as is often the case, parties are related or are close friends, the question of inheritance may arise. Where it can actually be proved that one party survived the other even by seconds, then rights may pass from one estate to the other. Proof only requires the normal civil standard of balance of probability. Suppose John and Jean are both killed in a common calamity. John has made a will leaving everything to Jean. If John dies first, his estate vests in Jean and there is no minimum period of time required for her survivorship. It might only be a matter of seconds. John's estate forms part of her estate and will be divided among her heirs. However, if Jean dies before John, she acquires no vested right and John's estate will be divided according to the rules of intestate succession, unless the will contains a "whom failing" provision.

If there is no proof, certain presumptions will be used. Under common law, there was no presumption and both parties were presumed to have died at exactly the same time. This meant that there could be no passing of property from one estate to the other. In *Ross's J.F. v Martin*, 1955 S.C. (HL) 56, two sisters had "mirror-image" wills leaving everything to the other, whom failing to a named charity. They both died as a result of a gas leak and there was no indication as to which had died first. Because, at common law, neither had survived the other, the "whom failing" provision of their wills could not operate. Both of their estates had to be divided according to intestate succession, which meant that the charity had no claim. Clearly this interpretation did not achieve the result the sisters would have wished.

The severity of the common law has given way to a kinder presumption under the 1964 Act. It provides that where two people die in circumstances which suggest simultaneous death, or which make it uncertain, the general rule is that the younger person is presumed to have survived the elder. To put it another way, the older person dies first. There are two important exceptions to this simple general rule:

(1) Where the parties were spouses or civil partners, the presumption is that they died simultaneously and that neither survived the other. In effect, this means that their estates are divided as though they had been single people.

(2) If the older person made a bequest in favour of the younger person, whom failing to a third party and the younger person is intestate (or partially intestate), the

older party, for the purpose of that bequest only, is presumed to have survived the younger. All the conditions in the previous sentence have to be fulfilled if this particular presumption is to be applied. Thus if the younger party died testate, or if there was no "whom failing" provision, the normal presumption would apply and the elder would be deemed to have died first. Although this provision seems complicated it was designed to protect the potential position of the "whom failing" legatee rather than allow the elder party's bequest to go to the younger party's heirs in intestacy.

A practical example may help to clarify the issues. Gretta and Christine are unmarried sisters, Gretta being the elder of the two. Their only living relative is their brother John. Whilst out for a run in their car, the sisters collide with an oncoming lorry. When the emergency services arrive, they are both pronounced dead. Gretta has a will, leaving everything to Christine, whom failing John. Christine died intestate. How will Gretta and Christine's estates be divided? Would it have made any difference if Christine had made a will leaving everything to Gretta?

As a matter of pure fact, there is no proof as to which died first, thus the statutory presumptions will apply. Whilst the elder is normally presumed to have died first, in this case the presumption is reversed because the elder made a bequest in favour of the younger, who died intestate, whom failing a third party (John), i.e. Christine dies first. As Christine died before Gretta, Christine could not have any vested right in Gretta's estate, so John inherits under the "whom failing" provision.

However, in respect of the second question, if Christine had made a will, the normal presumption about survivorship would apply and Gretta, the older sister, would die first; her estate would then vest in Christine. Christine's estate, including the vested right to Gretta's estate, would have to be dealt with according to the rules of intestate succession, since the only provision in the will has failed. Thus, everything goes to John. (The rules of intestate succession are explained in Chapter 4.)

In one sense, the end result is very similar in both cases in that everything finds its way to John. However, the actual administration of the estates is going to be very different. Many modern wills provide that a beneficiary must survive the testator for, say, 30 days to avoid a double passing of property within a short period of time.

Up to this point it has been presumed that only two people die in a common calamity. In practice there could be more, but the 1964 Act only deals with "twos". Thus, if three members of a family die in a tragic common calamity, it is necessary to apply the presumptions between them in twos.

---

3. LEGAL RIGHTS

INTRODUCTION

Legal rights are of very ancient origin in Scots law. Their application over the centuries has meant that it is not possible to disinherit totally one's spouse (now including civil partner) or children. This is a somewhat different tradition from what existed until relatively recently in English law. Although legal rights in Scotland are now statutory under the 1964 Act, that statute merely modernised them, whilst retaining much of the old common law provisions and vocabulary.

Strictly speaking, legal rights are not rights of succession so much as debts due from the deceased's estate (*Naismyth v Boyes* (1899) 1 F. (HL) 79). It should also be noted that in an *intestate* estate, a surviving spouse or civil partner may also claim prior rights (explained in Chapter 4) which rank after debts but before legal rights. However, legal rights only rank against the net moveable estate. Net moveable estate is the amount left after all debts, funeral expenses and legal and administrative costs of winding up and dividing the estate have been met and prior rights (where appropriate) are also satisfied. Thus, in practice, legal rights rank in second or third place against the moveable estate, depending on circumstances.

Legal rights are fixed at the moment of death. They are not affected by subsequent increases or decreases in the value of the estate or by additional funds or property, such as income and dividends, subsequently coming in to the executry. Interest is deemed to accrue in the claimant's favour from date of death to date of payment at "prudent management" rate. Legal rights can, and do, arise in both intestate and testate succession. Even if the deceased left a will, it is not possible to defeat legal rights by a testamentary provision. However, it is possible for anyone to minimise the amount from which legal rights can be claimed. One possibility is to convert as much as possible of his moveable property into heritage. In this way, the amount available for legal rights is obviously minimised. Another possibility would be to purchase an annuity, which dies with the person entitled to it.

CATEGORIES OF LEGAL RIGHTS

There are two legal rights: relict's part and legitim, to give them their ancient and traditional titles. It seems likely that the old titles will disappear in favour of the generic term "legal rights".

Relict's part

This was traditionally known either as *jus relictae* (right of the widow) or *jus relicti* (right of the widower). The surviving spouse (and, where applicable, this now includes a civil partner) can claim one half of the deceased's net moveable estate, where there are no children or direct descendants of children. If there are children or descendants of predeceasing children, the relict may claim one third of the net moveable estate. Relict's part is only available to a spouse or civil partner. The 2006 Act has introduced certain rights of succession to a cohabitee, but these are not the same as *jus relictae* or *jus relicti*.

Under the pre-2006 law a cohabitee could sometimes claim full legal rights if that cohabitee claimed successfully to have been irregularly married to the deceased by cohabitation with habit and repute. Such a marriage can only be legally recognised by a declarator of the Court of Session. The parties must have cohabited for a reasonable period of time and must have been generally reputed to be husband and wife. Many cohabiting couples nowadays make it publicly known that they are not married, so irregular marriage had no relevance for them. Equally, it had no relevance to people of the same sex who cohabited. Irregular marriage is being phased out by the 2006 Act. Any period of cohabitation which began before the Act came into force on May 4, 2006 can still be taken into account in any claim to be irregularly married, even when the period ends or continues after the date of commencement. There is also provision to recognise as valid a marriage entered into abroad where, unknown to the parties, the marriage was invalid under the law of that country.

There is really no such thing as a "common law spouse" and the expression is best avoided. The same applies to the curious term "significant other person", so beloved of officialdom. The 2006 Act gave groundbreaking rights to cohabiting couples, which are explained, insofar as they apply to intestate succession, in Chapter 4. It is important, however, to understand that the rights of a surviving cohabitee are very different from those of a surviving spouse or civil partner.

Legitim

Legitim, or "bairn's part", is the right of surviving children, or the direct descendants of predeceasing children, to claim against a fund made up of one half of the net moveable estate where there is no surviving spouse or civil partner. If there is a surviving spouse or civil partner, the legitim fund will be one third of the net moveable estate.

Before the 1964 Act came into force, only children who actually survived the deceased could have any claim against the legitim fund. This rule was logical in that it simply applied the basic rule of succession that a party can only succeed to the estate of a deceased person if he survives that person. However, the application of the rule lead to perceived injustice, since grandchildren were unable to make any claim to the legal rights which their predeceasing parent could have enjoyed. The 1964 Act introduced the concept of "representation", which allows children of a predeceasing child to claim their late parent's share. Thus if A dies and his descendants are child C and grandchildren E and F, the children of a predeceasing child D, the legitim fund is divided into two parts. One half goes to C and the other half is shared equally between E and F, who represent their predeceasing parent D.

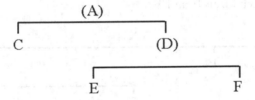

"Children" includes not only those born within marriage but also illegitimate and adopted children. Under the Law Reform (Miscellaneous Provisions) (Scotland) Act 1968, illegitimate children were given the right to claim against a parent's estate. The Law Reform (Parent and Child) (Scotland) Act 1986 virtually abolished the distinction between legitimate and illegitimate children but, somewhat confusingly, retained the illegitimacy status. The 2006 Act, section 21, finally abolishes this status, subject to exceptions in respect of succeeding to coats-of-arms or titles.

Under the 1964 Act, adopted children are placed in the same position as natural children of their adoptive parents. Any rights of succession an adopted child might have against his actual physical parents are extinguished. At common law, the position of an adopted child was bleak. Because he was regarded as a *filius nullius* (son of no one) he had no rights of succession against either adoptive or natural parents (*Clarke v Carfin Coal Co.* (1891) 18 R. (HL) 63). This injustice was gradually subject to statutory inroads, culminating in the 1964 provisions. The pre-1964 Act law still applies to titles and coats-of-arms. Step-children do not have any claim on the legitim fund of a step-parent.

DIVISION OF THE LEGITIM FUND

The manner in which the legitim fund is distributed among the claimants may be *per capita* (by head) or *per stirpes* (by branch). Where the division is *per capita*, the fund is divided equally among all the claimants. This type of division occurs when *all* the claimants are in the same relationship to the deceased. Thus, if all the claimants are surviving children, they share on a *per capita* basis. If all children have predeceased and the claimants are grandchildren, these grandchildren are all in the same relationship to the deceased and will share *per capita* in the fund. However, if the claimants are not all in the same degree, the division is *per stirpes*. An example may clarify: suppose X (the deceased) had four children, A, B, C and D. B and D survive their parent, A predeceases leaving no children and C also predeceases, but leaving two children E and F.

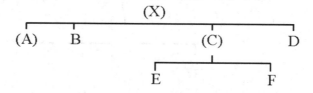

The branch is worked out by finding the collateral line of succession nearest to the deceased where there is at least one living claimant. A "collateral" is a person who shares an ancestor but whose succession is not in the same direct line as another claimant. Thus siblings are collaterals, because they share parents, as are cousins, who share grandparents. In this case, the collateral line of succession nearest to the parent is clearly that of children. Party A has predeceased, leaving no children. There is no claim that can be made on his behalf, since only his direct descendants could represent. Accordingly, the fund is divided into three branches. Children B and D each take a complete branch. The remaining branch, which would have belonged to child C, is claimed by grandchildren E and F through representation and is shared equally between the two of them.

COLLATION *INTER LIBEROS*

If a person wishes to make a claim on the legitim fund but, during the lifetime of the deceased, he received advances or gifts of moveable property, he must collate (add back) the amount of such gifts or advances into the legitim fund. The fund is then divided *inter liberos* (among the children) in the normal way. This is, in fact, a paper exercise since money is not literally paid back into the fund. It is merely taken into account in making the calculation of any division. An example may clarify: X, a widower, dies, leaving three children, P, Q and R. The net moveable estate is £60,000 which means that, as there is no surviving spouse, the legitim fund is £30,000. Three years before his death, X gave £6,000 in cash to P. If P wishes to claim, he must collate the £6,000. This means that the legitim fund is actually £36,000 for the purposes of calculation. The fund will then be divided in the normal way among the three claimants *per capita*, giving each of them £12,000. Since P has already had £6,000 to account, he will receive a further £6,000, bringing his total share up to £12,000. Q and R will each receive £12,000 in the normal way.

There could be cases where a child has received a substantial advance and could actually be out of pocket if he were to claim legitim. He would be well advised not to make a claim, in which case he does not require to collate. In *Coats' Trs v Coats*, 1914 S.C. 744, the only claimant on the legitim fund had received advances, but these were smaller than the substantial advances made to her siblings. The claimant failed in her attempt to require her siblings to collate their advances. Sums of money expended in normal parental maintenance and provision of education need not be collated nor need loans made to a child, as these are more in the nature of a debt due to the estate.

It is important to note that collation only applies to advances of moveable property. Thus if, say, a child is given actual heritable property, that does not require to be collated and he can make a full claim on the legitim fund. If, on the other hand, the child was given a sum of money to buy a house, that sum is clearly moveable and would require to be collated. Occasionally a parent may provide in his will that a particular advance does not require to be collated for the purposes of legitim claims, although this is unusual as most wills make provisions in lieu of legitim.

RENUNCIATION OF LEGITIM

It is always open to any person entitled to claim legal rights to renounce his claim on the legitim fund. This has a different effect on the position of other claimants depending on whether the renunciation takes place before or after the death of the parent.

If the discharge or renunciation takes place before the death of the parent, that claimant is deemed, for this purpose only, to have died before his parent and to have left no issue to represent him, irrespective of the true facts. Since the legitim fund is a constant factor, the obvious result of this renunciation is that the amount available to other claimants is bound to increase. In *Obers v Paton's Trs* (1897) 24 R. 719, P, a Scot, was declared bankrupt in France. When his father was dying, P discharged his claim to legitim. Assuming P survived his father (which he did) this had the effect of increasing the amount available to his siblings and reducing the amount potentially available to his creditors. This was an astute move, but the court reduced (nullified) the discharge as it was a gratuitous alienation at common law made to the prejudice of his creditors.

However, if (as is more usual) the discharge takes place after the death of the parent, the effect is quite different. As already stated, legal rights are fixed at the moment of death and nothing which takes place after the death can affect the amount designated for each claimant. In such a case, the portion of the legitim fund which has been renounced falls into the free estate or residue of the estate. It is not added to the share of other claimants against the fund. An example will clarify: Jack dies, leaving a widow Jill and two children, Bill and Ben. If the net moveable estate amounts to £18,000, Jill is entitled to one third, by way of *jus relictae* (£6,000) and the legitim fund is of the same amount. If Ben renounced his claim to legal rights before Jack died, Ben would be treated as having died before his father and without leaving any children of his own. Ben would thus be discounted as far as the calculation of legal rights is concerned and the entire legitim fund of £6,000 would go to Bill. If, however, Ben discharges his claim on the fund after the death of Jack, the outcome would be different. Because legal rights are fixed at the moment of death, Bill's share of the legitim fund cannot be increased and he will only receive one half of the fund (£3,000), just as if Ben had accepted his share. The £3,000 which Ben has rejected will fall into the free estate or residue.

Spouses, civil partners and children cannot be deprived of legal rights but they may be required to choose or elect between such rights and a legacy in their provision. This legal principle is named "approbate and reprobate" which, in simple terms, means that it is not possible for someone both to accept and reject the same document. Put more colloquially, a claimant cannot "have his cake and eat it too".

Unless there is express provision to the contrary, in all wills made after the 1964 Act came into force, any provision in favour of spouses, civil partners or children is deemed to be in full and final settlement of legal rights. It does not matter whether the legacy provision is of heritable or moveable property or both, nor whether the provision is more or less generous than legal rights; the same principle applies. In effect, accepting a legacy provision, by statutory implication, serves as a renunciation of legal rights after the death of the parent. Thus if there are two children and each is left property in the parent's will but one elects to take legal rights, he receives only one half of the notional legitim fund. It is possible for a will to provide that a beneficiary will not lose his right to claim legal rights by accepting a legacy but such a provision is uncommon.

Although lawyers use the expression "legitim fund", this fund is really artificial as it is not kept in a separate account. Indeed, it is only in the later stages of the administration that a precise calculation of the legitim fund can be made, since debts and outlays can normally only be known accurately at this stage. Claiming legal rights against an intestate estate does not involve any formality since it is a basic entitlement. In a testate estate, the executor (or solicitor acting for him) would normally intimate a legacy to the person entitled to it. If that beneficiary is a person who could claim legal rights in lieu of a legacy, it is open to him to do so. He would normally be required to put his claim—and the renunciation of the legacy—in writing but there is no statutory style prescribed. It should be stressed that claiming legal rights rather than a legacy provision does not create intestacy. Sometimes members of a family may be reluctant to claim legal rights rather than a legacy, in the mistaken belief that it will require some kind of court action and that, in some way, the will may have to be contested. There is much scope for misunderstanding in this area and it merely underlines how important it is for members of a family to seek competent advice on an individual basis.

Legal rights will prescribe if they are not claimed within 20 years of their becoming enforceable.

---

4. INTESTATE SUCCESSION

A person is said to be "intestate" when he dies without leaving a will or other testamentary writing to direct how his estate is to be

distributed after his death. However, this is not the only occasion
where the rules of intestate succession are applied. The deceased
could have left a will which is wholly or partly ineffective. Strictly
speaking, the deceased could not be described as intestate, yet the
failure of the will means that the estate (or part of it) will have to
be wound up according to the rules of intestate succession. In some
cases, a will may only dispose of part of an estate and the
remainder has to be administered as though the deceased had died
intestate; this is referred to as a "partial intestacy".

The lay person often assumes, wrongly, that the division of an
estate under the rules of intestate succession is bound to be more
complicated than where there is a will giving clear instructions. In
fact, it is not administratively any more difficult to divide an
intestate estate. In some ways it is easier as executors have no will
to interpret, virtually no discretion and must simply apply the rules.
The problem is much more social, in that the rules of division in
intestacy may well not reflect what the deceased's real wishes
would have been. Assuming payment of lawful debts and funeral
expenses, the division of an intestate estate has to be considered in
three successive stages. Not all stages are relevant in every estate,
but the division would have to follow the order of (1) prior rights,
(2) legal rights and (3) dead's part. Stages (1) and (3) are now
examined in detail. Legal rights have already been examined in
Chapter 3.

PRIOR RIGHTS

There are three elements to a claim for prior rights, but before
considering these, three important points should be noted:

(1) Prior rights *only* apply in intestate succession. They are
    not like legal rights, which can be claimed against a testate
    estate.
(2) Prior rights, as the name suggests, must be met first out of
    the intestate estate (after payment of debts) and before
    any legal rights can be calculated, far less distributed. The
    maximum amounts that may be claimed are reviewed
    regularly and those shown in this book were last updated
    in 2005.
(3) Prior rights are only available to a surviving spouse or civil
    partner. They are not available to cohabitees, whose
    position is outlined at the end of this chapter.

As is the case with claims for legal rights, occasionally situations
arise where a surviving party may wish to prove an irregular

marriage to the deceased, in order to make a claim. Given the abolition of irregular marriage under the 2006 Act, this possibility has declining relevance. Children have no rights of representation in respect of the prior rights of a predeceasing parent.

Dwellinghouse right

Under section 8(1) of the 1964 Act, the surviving spouse or civil partner is entitled to the ownership or tenancy of any one house (which includes a flatted residence) owned or tenanted by the deceased at the time of death. The house also includes any garden ground and pertinents, but not moveable property, at least under this heading. It is essential, however, that the surviving spouse or civil partner was ordinarily resident in the house in question at the time of the intestate's death. However, it does not matter whether or not the deceased was ordinarily resident in the house.

The maximum value of this benefit is £300,000 at the time of writing. This figure is increased from time to time by statutory instrument to take account of inflation, as are the amounts in the other two benefits outlined. If the deceased's interest in the house is more than £300,000, the survivor is entitled to a sum of £300,000 only. In such situations, members of the family may be able to come to an arrangement whereby the surviving spouse retains the house but buys back any amount in excess of the maximum figure.

If the house forms part of subjects included within a tenancy or where it forms part of subjects used by the deceased for the purposes of a trade, profession or occupation (such as a farm house), a cash sum in lieu would normally be payable.

The surviving spouse or civil partner has to take the house under the same terms as were enjoyed by the deceased. The majority of houses owned by married couples are held in joint names of husband and wife. The same probably applies to civil partners. In such a case, the surviving spouse or civil partner can (obviously) only take the share belonging to the deceased. In addition, the house, or share, is taken subject to any existing right of security. Thus if a house worth £190,000 is in the sole name of the deceased but is subject to a standard security for £100,000, only the equity of the house, namely a value £90,000, passes to the survivor. As explained in Chapter 1, the proceeds of an insurance policy count as a moveable asset and are not automatically offset against a heritable debt.

In a substantial number of cases, a house may be held not only in joint names of husband and wife (or civil partners), but also in joint names of husband, wife and survivor. This arrangement is known as a special destination and is explained in more detail in Chapter 10. The effect of a special destination in a heritable title is to move the deceased's share, at the moment of death, to the survivor(s) without further legal formality. When this takes place, the dwelling house right has no relevance and, in cases where the deceased's share is worth more than £300,000, would actually leave the survivor in a more advantageous position.

Occasionally, the deceased may have owned more than one house in which the survivor was ordinarily resident at the time of his death, e.g. a second home. In this case, the survivor has six months in which to elect (choose) which house to take.

Furniture right

Under section 8(3) of the 1964 Act, the surviving spouse or civil partner is entitled to receive the deceased's share in the furniture and plenishings from the dwellinghouse in which the survivor was ordinarily resident, up to a value of £24,000. As with the dwellinghouse right, it does not matter whether the deceased was normally resident in the house. The value is what the furniture is worth, not what it would cost to replace it of new. Where the value of the deceased's share of the furniture is more than £24,000, the survivor may select items up to a value of £24,000. The furniture right applies even although the house itself is not part of the intestate estate, as would happen when the heritable property passed under a special destination. The furniture right applies equally where the house was not owned by the deceased, e.g. where it was rented, always provided that the surviving spouse was ordinarily resident in it at the time of the deceased's death.

If two or more houses are involved, the survivor must, within six months of the death of the intestate, elect which lot of furniture to take. It seems that the furniture can only be taken from one house and the survivor is not allowed a pick and mix from the two.

As well as including the most obvious categories such as furniture, carpets and curtains, the plenishings include (and the list is not exhaustive) "garden effects, domestic animals, plate, plated articles, linen, china, glass, books, pictures, prints, articles of household use and consumable stores". There is no mention of motor cars and professional practice is not to include a car as part of the furniture.

Excluded from furniture and plenishings are animals used for business purposes, money, securities and heirlooms. What might be included within the categories of heirlooms is, to use Professor Michael Meston's words, "magnificently vague". It is intended to cover items which, because of their associations rather than their value, ought to pass to the members of the deceased's family other than the surviving spouse. If these items are of purely sentimental value, this is unlikely to be contentious but if they are more valuable, the executor could be put in a somewhat difficult position.

Financial provision
It is provided in section 9 of the 1964 Act that, after the dwellinghouse and furniture rights have been satisfied, there is a financial provision entitling the survivor to the sum of £75,000 where the deceased left no surviving children or representatives of predeceasing children. If there are surviving children or representatives, the sum is £42,000.

If, as is quite frequently the case, there is not enough left to meet the financial provision in full, the entire remaining estate, heritable and/or moveable, is made over to the survivor in full and final satisfaction. If there is adequate to pay the monetary right in full but both heritable and moveable property are left in the estate after satisfaction of the dwellinghouse and furniture rights, the sum of £75,000/£42,000 will be paid proportionately out of the remaining heritable and moveable estate. This is illustrated in the second of the two practical illustrations given towards the end of this chapter.

If there is only partial intestacy and the survivor is entitled to a legacy from the estate, the financial provision must be set off against the amount of the legacy. The dwellinghouse and furniture rights do not require to be set off in this way.

It is worth noting that the three prior rights, although obviously considered under the one heading are, in fact, independent of one another and not merely part of a cash fund. So, in many ways, what a survivor receives is pot luck and depends purely on the mixture of assets in the estate. If someone leaves a house worth £60,000, furniture worth £500 and investments of £200,000, the prior rights (in total) would be less than an estate with a house valued at £130,000, furniture of £1,000 and investments of £20,000, although the former estate in total is greater in value than the latter.

If any surplus of moveable property is left after payment of prior rights, the next stage would be calculation of legal rights.

LEGAL RIGHTS

Legal rights have already been covered in some detail in Chapter 3 and it is not necessary to go over the same ground twice. It is worth underlining once again the fact that the legal rights can only be claimed from the net moveable estate, i.e. after payment of lawful debts *and* satisfaction of any prior rights. In many smaller estates, the prior rights of the surviving spouse or civil partner will, in fact, exhaust the entire estate, leaving nothing to be claimed under legal rights.

DEAD'S PART

The balance that remains after the satisfaction of both prior and legal rights is the free estate or "dead's part". It may contain heritable and moveable property. From what has already been demonstrated, it stands to reason that if someone dies intestate, with no surviving spouse, civil partner or children, his entire estate is dead's part.

It is crucial to understand that dead's part can only be claimed in the event of intestacy. A claim to dead's part is *not* like a claim for legal rights which can, as already shown, prevail against a will. Thus, siblings and other members of the family have no claim to dead's part if the deceased made a valid will. It might be upsetting if, say, a brother, who never married, entered a civil partnership or fathered any children, leaves all his property to the local Cats' Home but, in such circumstances, his sister has no legal claim of succession to any part of the estate.

The 1964 Act lays down the order of succession to the dead's part. In essence, it is simple: the executor will look at each successive "class" of relations in the under-noted list. As soon as he strikes a class in which there is a possible claimant, he stops there and goes no further. This is the class to whom, or among whom, the dead's part falls to be divided. Representation applies, unless indicated to the contrary. There is no provision for cohabitees, whose position is outlined below. The rules on division *per capita* or *per stirpes* are exactly the same as for legal rights.

The order of distribution is as follows:

(1) children;
(2) parents (no representation) *and* siblings (provided there is at least one survivor from each class)—each class shares one half of the free estate;
(3) siblings (where there is no surviving parent);
(4) parents (where there are no surviving siblings)—there is no representation;
(5) surviving spouse (no representation);
(6) uncles and aunts—maternal or paternal;
(7) grandparents;
(8) collaterals of grandparents;
(9) remoter ancestors;
(10) the Crown.

The effect of this list is that there is representation in respect of the descending and collateral lines, but none in respect of parents and spouses. Collaterals (such as brothers and sisters or uncles and aunts) of the full blood (sharing both parents with the intestate or an ancestor) exclude those of the half blood (sharing one parent with the intestate or an ancestor). However, in the case of half blood, it makes no difference whether the shared parent was mother or father. A step-brother or step-sister has no claim on the estate. Intestate succession still favours blood relationship. Subject to the two exceptions to representation, it does not matter how remote the blood relationship is, nor does it matter whether it was legitimate or illegitimate, to use the older concepts. If, after working through the above list, no relation can be found, the estate will go to the Crown as *ultimus haeres* (final heir). An official with the impressive title of the Queen's and Lord Treasurer's Remembrancer takes possession of the estate and does not require to obtain confirmation to do so. He will advertise for possible relatives, pay debts and apply the balance to the Treasury. In carrying out his duties, the Remembrancer has an element of discretion, not open to an executor of an intestate estate. For example, he could make a financial payment to, say, a companion or retainer of the deceased.

Because prior rights may eat into an estate it is possible, as already noted, that there may not be sufficient to satisfy legal rights, far less any distribution of the dead's part. Indeed, there is a strange quirk in the law in that sometimes a surviving spouse could be better off under intestacy than being left everything under the deceased spouse's will. In the case of *Kerr, Petr*, 1968 S.L.T. (Sh. Ct) 61, a widow was left all of her husband's relatively modest estate. There were no other bequests under the will. The children of the marriage wished to claim their legal rights. If they were to succeed, obviously less of the estate would be available to the widow. If the husband had died intestate, the widow's prior rights would have exhausted the entire estate. The widow decided to disclaim her benefit under the will. As her legacy was the only provision, the estate fell into intestacy. She then claimed her prior rights and received the entire estate. The children could still, as a matter of law, claim legal rights but as there were no remaining funds to meet them, these rights were worth precisely nothing. It is an interesting concept that, in law, parties can have an absolute right to something which is of no value. That, however, is a matter for scholars of jurisprudence to ponder. The above case is an unusual one that, in the writer's view, does not undermine the general advice that it is normally prudent to leave a will rather than rely on intestacy. Nevertheless, in *Kerr* the result of putting the estate into intestacy certainly had the effect of carrying out the testator's real wishes. The device only worked because there was no other provision in the will. If the will had left everything to the wife, whom failing the children (which would be more usual), the wife's renunciation of the legacy would not have pushed the estate into intestacy and she would only have been able to claim legal rights.

EXAMPLES OF DIVISION OF INTESTATE ESTATES

Example 1
A husband dies leaving a widow and two children. His net estate is £215,100 made up of dwellinghouse (£160,000), furniture (£4,100) and investments of £51,000.

	Heritable	Moveable
Dwellinghouse	160,000	
Furniture		4,100
Investments		51,000
	160,000	55,100
Deduct prior rights		
Dwellinghouse	160,000	
Furniture		4,100
Financial provision		42,000
Balances	Nil	9,000
Deduct legal rights		
Relict's part		3,000
Legitim		3,000
Balances	Nil	3,000
Deduct dead's part		3,000
Balances	Nil	Nil

The final distribution would be:
Widow

Prior Rights	206,100	
Relict's part	3,000	
		209,100

Son

Legitim (half share)	1,500	
Dead's part (half share)	1,500	
		3,000

Daughter

Legitim (half share)	1,500	
Dead's part (half share)	1,500	
		3,000
		215,100

The above example is one of classic simplicity. Notice that even in this case, where there are sufficient funds to make a legitim payment, the lion's share of the estate passes to the widow.

Example 2

In this second example, the family circumstances are the same, as is the total amount of the net estate, but there is a second heritable property, a holiday home.

	Heritable	Moveable
Dwellinghouse	100,000	
Furniture		4,100
Holiday home	60,000	
Investments		51,000
	160,000	55,100

Deduct prior rights

	Heritable	Moveable
Dwellinghouse	100,000	
Furniture		4,100
Balances	*60,000*	*51,000*
Financial Provision (*see explanation below*)	22,680	19,320
Balances	37,320	31,680

Deduct legal rights

	Heritable	Moveable
Relict's part		10,560
Legitim		10,560
Balances	37,320	10,560

Deduct dead's part	37,320	10,560
Balances	Nil	Nil

The fact that there is a mixture of heritable and moveable property left after the dwellinghouse and furniture rights have been satisfied means that the financial provision has to be met proportionately out of the balances (shown in *italics* purely for illustration), i.e. in a ratio of 60,000/51,000 which, expressed as a percentage, is 54/46. Thus 54 per cent of £42,000 is taken from the heritable estate and 46 per cent from the moveable: £22,680 and £19,320 respectively. The fact that the dead's part also contains a heritable and moveable balance does not create any problem, at least on paper, as the value will simply be halved between the two children.

The final distribution would be:

Widow

Prior Rights	146,100	
Relict's part	10,560	
		156,660

Son

Legitim (half share)	5,280	
Dead's part (half share)	23,940	
		29,200

Daughter

Legitim (half share)	5,280	
Dead's part (half share)	23,940	
		29,220
Total estate		215,100

COHABITING COUPLES

There is nothing new about couples cohabiting. However, relationships between couples have become more complex over the last 50 years or so. Subject to the exception of irregular marriage, it was normally clear whether couples were married or not. If they were married, there were rights of succession, but not otherwise. To all intents and purposes, same-sex couples who have entered a civil partnership are in a virtually identical position to married couples when it comes to succession. However, there is no legal form of partnership available for members of the opposite sex who cohabit but are not legally married or for members of the same sex who live together as partners, but are not civil partners. The 2006 Act (section 29) makes provision for these situations for the first time. For the purposes of succession and certain other rights of property (section 25), a cohabitant is described as a person who is or was living with another person as if they were husband and wife, or two persons of the same sex who are or were living together as if they were civil partners. The Act then goes on to list a number of factors which the court should have regard to, namely:

(1) the length of the period during which the two persons lived together;
(2) the nature of their relationship during that period; and
(3) the nature and extent of any financial arrangements subsisting, or which subsisted, during that period.

Cohabitants can now make a claim on their partner's estate if their partner died without leaving a valid will. If the deceased cohabitant has made a will, then the law is unchanged and a cohabitant would not be entitled to claim any financial provision from the deceased's estate, other than any legacy in the will. (At the time of writing, the Scottish Law Commission is considering the possibility of cohabitants' rights to claim against a testate estate.)

However, in the event of intestacy, application may be made to the court by the surviving cohabitant for an award to be made. The award may take the form of a capital sum or property transfer order and is at the discretion of the court, taking relevant circumstances, as defined by the Act, into account, such as the size of the estate, other benefits received (such as the proceeds of a life assurance policy) and other claims on the estate. Any capital payment can be made by instalments.

Significantly, the surviving cohabitee is not entitled to a larger amount than s/he would have been entitled to if the parties had been married or in a civil partnership. Furthermore, any payments must be made from the deceased's net estate after payment of inheritance tax, debts and satisfaction of any prior or legal rights claims of a surviving spouse or civil partner. It is particularly important to note that there is a six month time limit from the death of the intestate partner to raise these claims. There is no judicial discretion to extend this period. Furthermore, the parties must have actually been cohabiting in Scotland at the time of the death.

At the time of writing, this aspect of the law is still new and has not been subject to judicial interpretation.

EXECUTORS

The office of executor will be considered further in Chapter 12 but
some preliminary comments are required at this stage. The executor is the person who ingathers the estate of the deceased, pays
debts and then distributes the estate to those entitled to it. The
office, like that of a trustee, is gratuitous.

If the deceased left a will, he should also have made arrangements in that will for the appointment of an executor, who has the
resulting title of executor-nominate. However, if the estate is
intestate, or if the will made no such provisions, the court will have
to appoint an executor, who is given the title of executor-dative.

In order for an executor-dative to be appointed, an application
has to be lodged in the form of a petition to the sheriff court of the
sheriffdom in which the deceased was domiciled. Generally speaking, parties are not in competition with one another to be
appointed to this office, although occasionally sibling rivalry will
rear its head. In *Russo v Russo*, 1998 S.L.T. (Sh. Ct) 32, a widow
died leaving three sons, one of whom had been decerned
(appointed) as executor-dative, but had not been confirmed to the
estate. One of the other sons also wished to be appointed joint
executor. The sheriff principal agreed that the appointment of an
executor-dative was an administrative and not a judicial function.
The court had no discretion to choose between two brothers of the
same blood.

The parties entitled to appointment are, in order of priority:

(1) The surviving spouse, if that spouse has prior rights which
     exhaust the estate;
(2) the deceased's next-of-kin (relations entitled to succeed
     under intestate succession);
(3) other persons in the order in which they are entitled to
     succeed according to the rules of intestate succession;
(4) creditors of the deceased;
(5) legatees;
(6) the procurator fiscal or a judicial factor.

At common law, "next-of-kin" referred to the class nearest in
degree to the deceased, which had at least one surviving member.
It would be perfectly in order for a surviving spouse, particularly if
elderly, to decline the office and for, say, the eldest son to petition
for appointment. In cases where there are two or more applicants
within the same category, they are all entitled to be appointed
jointly.

The lay person often fails to appreciate that the appointment of
an executor does not permit that person to intromit (uplift, dispose

or distribute) with the estate. Whether executor-nominate or executor-dative, he must apply to the sheriff for "confirmation". Put simply, this is an inventory of the items in the deceased's estate and gives the executor legal title to intromit with the estate as listed. More is said about confirmation in Chapter 12. Anyone taking the law into his own hands without being appointed as executor and being confirmed will be classed as a "vitious intromitter" and may be held liable for all the debts of the deceased. This could be the case even when there was no actual fraudulent intention.

An executor-dative is required to lodge a bond of caution (pronounced "kay-shun") with the sheriff that he will make the estate "furthcoming", i.e. that he will hand it over to those entitled to it. Such a bond is normally provided by an insurance company in return for a single premium payment. However, under section 5 of the Law Reform (Miscellaneous Provisions) (Scotland) Act 1980 a bond of caution is not required when a surviving spouse inherits the entire estate through prior rights.

---

5. ESSENTIAL AND FORMAL VALIDITY

Many a good story, whether taken from the classics or popular yarns, centres around a will. Did the deceased make a will? If so, where is it? If he made such a will, was he sane when he made it? Why, if he was sane, did he decide to leave all his money to the Cats' Home? Is the deceased trying to get even with his family from beyond the grave?

The reader may even have seen old "B" movies which feature a formal reading of the will, usually on a wet afternoon after the funeral and often bringing an unpleasant surprise to the members of the deceased's family by naming an entirely unexpected main beneficiary. It becomes clear that this beneficiary is the party who will be murdered and, obviously, suspicion will fall on the "heir apparent", who was disappointed by the will. Such formal readings of a will virtually never take place in practice, although these occasions would make great theatre.

As stated in the previous chapter, the average lay person might perceive that there will be fewer complications in the event of someone dying testate than intestate. This has an element of truth in it, but it is not the whole truth. If a party dies intestate, the rules

of intestate succession have to be applied. It has been demonstrated that there are few grey areas in the rules of intestate
succession and there is little or no room for flexibility, subject to
the judicial discretion which may be applied in the case of a
surviving cohabitee.

In the case of testate succession, there is the obvious advantage
that people know where they stand. It makes sense to have a clear
will, professionally framed and properly signed, and then to ensure
that it is regularly updated. The great majority of wills present no
problems and prevent many from arising. Yet there is more
potential for matters to go wrong, even if this only happens in a
small minority of cases. Most estates falling under testate succession are wound up uneventfully. Nevertheless anyone working in
the legal environment always has to be prepared for the
unexpected.

The law of testate succession deals with the disposal, on death,
of property by means of a will or other testamentary writing. If a
will creates a trust, this trust continues beyond the actual executry
of the estate and the document is usually known as a trust
disposition and settlement, referred to in professional jargon as a
"TD and S".

One obvious problem with testate succession is that no two wills
are ever identical, even if they are very similar. It is important,
when making a will, that testators consider as many eventualities as
possible, even those which may be less pleasant. Parents do not
normally expect to outlive their children, but there is no guarantee
in life how events will turn out. It may be painful to consider a
child, or other younger beneficiary, predeceasing, but it is always a
possibility. Traditionally, the average married man assumes that he
will die before his wife. It *is* still the case that men have shorter
lives (from an actuarial viewpoint) than women, but people do not
always die in what might be seen as the natural order.

There are few actual rules about what people cannot do by will.
It was demonstrated in Chapter 3 that no one can exclude valid
claims to legal rights by a spouse, civil partner or child(ren).

ESSENTIAL VALIDITY

A will, or testamentary settlement, is a *written* declaration of what a
person wishes to be done with his estate after death. There are no
special forms of words and the reader will have to look long and
hard to find any professionally drafted will which begins with the
words "I, being of sound mind and body . . ."; save that for the "B"
movies referred to above.

One of the most common failings in home-made wills is that often they import half-understood jargon from books, novels and films. In practice, it is much safer to refer to "children" than "issue", because issue means not only children but also all direct descendants. Yet, to some people, "issue" sounds more impressive. The other main failing concerns the formal validity of the document.

It is perfectly true that a will can competently be written on the back of a cigarette packet, although this is hardly the most respectful way of treating potential beneficiaries. Any document that gives rise to obligations requires to be signed; in other words it must be formally valid. This is different from a document being essentially valid, which concerns the essence of the document, e.g. what it purports to do, or it may refer to some external factor which is not immediately obvious, such as lack of capacity on the part of the granter.

The testator must have the necessary capacity in law to "test", i.e. to make a valid will. To put it another way, the law must recognise that he is able to dispose of property *mortis causa* (on account of death) at the time the will is made. Any person, male or female, aged 12 years or over can test (Age of Legal Capacity (Scotland) Act 1991, section 2(2)). Someone who is insane cannot form the necessary thought process to test. If the testator, though insane, had lucid intervals, he might still have the power to form the necessary intention, as in *Nisbet's Trs v Nisbet* (1871) 9 M. 937. A similar result could be found in cases of delusion and abnormal eccentricity. Generations of students have been introduced to the case of *Morrison v Maclean's Trs* (1862) 24 D. 625 where an eccentric testator's will was held to be valid, despite the fact that much of his everyday speech had been of an obscene and bizarre nature and that he claimed to have been fed from an eagle's nest when young.

The law presumes in favour of sanity unless the testator has been "sectioned" under mental health legislation, where insanity (even if only temporary insanity) is presumed. This presumption can be rebutted. Capacity to test might also be affected by facility and circumvention or undue influence.

"Facility" is not an easy state to define. It certainly falls short of insanity but it means that a person is easily manipulated by others. A facility might occur in someone who is elderly or feeble-minded (for whatever reason). In itself, a notional facility might not be enough to make a will invalid, particularly if the provisions of the will are clear in themselves. For the will to be open to challenge, there would also need to be an element of circumvention, i.e. literally "getting round" the testator to influence him to make certain testamentary provisions, in such a way as would be harmful to his interests.

Undue influence is different from facility and circumvention, but the distinction is sometimes easier to state than to draw. There is no need to show that the testator suffered any form of facility. Rather, there will be some relationship of trust and confidence between the beneficiary and the testator, even if this relationship need not be regarded as strictly fiduciary in law. Children can often influence their parents and vice versa—but a solicitor can influence his client, a doctor his patient, a minister a member of his congregation or even (as in *Honeyman's Exr v Sharp*, 1978 S.C. 223) an art dealer his customer. People can, of course, be influenced for good as much as for ill and the law does not seek to interfere in the giving of reasonable advice or counsel to potential testators. The possibility of challenge would only arise if it could be shown that a testator's intention had been in some way overborne. It is not surprising that the law is particularly severe on a solicitor who (contrary to his own professional ethics) draws up a client's will in his own favour. In such a case, the burden of proof that the bequest was reasonable would fall on the solicitor.

FORMAL VALIDITY

The first elementary, but crucial, matter to notice is that a will requires to be in writing. Even if someone, on his death bed, states that he is changing his will, this is of no significance unless the new provision is put into writing and properly signed as explained below. It is not possible (at least yet) to execute a valid will by means of recording other than writing, such as video tape or electronic communication.

The next obstacle to be cleared is whether the will was signed before August 1, 1995 or on or after this date. These two categories are now considered in turn.

Wills executed before August 1, 1995
There must still be a fair number of wills executed before the above date by people who are still alive. This means that the old law will continue to be relevant for a considerable period of time. Under the old law, a verbal nuncupative legacy of not more than £100 Scots (£8.33) was valid, but this provision is obsolete and has no modern relevance.

Pre-1995 practice was governed partly by common law and partly by ancient statute. The statutory provisions were found in a venerable collection of Acts of the Scots Parliament, interpreted over the years by the courts and partly modernised by 19th and 20th century legislation, known by the august collective title of the "Authentication Statutes".

Under the old law, before an executor can obtain confirmation on the basis of a will, which will requires to be in "probative form". This basically means that the court will presume that the execution (signature) of the document is valid, unless it can be proved to the contrary. In practice, it requires fairly convincing proof to overturn a probative document.

Attested will

The most usual form of probativity is where the will is attested, which means subscribed on every page and the signature on the last page witnessed by two individuals who confirm their witnessing by signature. (Probative documents other than wills did not require to be signed on every page.)

If there is an informality of execution, such as omitting to sign one of the pages, this would not normally be fatal to the validity of the will. It is possible to ask the court for this informality to be cured under the provisions of the Conveyancing (Scotland) Act 1874 section 39. This is generally known as "section 39 procedure". What the title lacks in originality it more than compensates when it comes to clarity.

In the case of *Williamson v Williamson*, 1997 S.L.T. 1044, Mrs Williamson had signed her will in 1988. The two witnesses were Mr Wilson and his wife. In a fit of absent-mindedness and in the heat of the moment, Mr Wilson accidentally signed his surname as "Williamson"; his wife managed to sign her name properly. After Mrs Williamson's death, a member of her family noticed this obvious inconsistency and challenged the validity of the will. Eventually, the will was declared to be invalid, as one of the witness' signatures was fatally flawed. This was deemed to be more than mere informality of execution and so was not curable under section 39 procedure. Mrs Williamson's estate fell into intestate succession. (If the witness had signed his correct name but had been wrongly designed in the testing clause, this would have been curable under section 39 procedure.) In *Braithwaite v Bank of Scotland*, 1997 G.W.D. 40–2037, a witness to a pre-1995 Act document, as a joke in poor taste, described himself falsely as a "consultant gynaecologist". Although, in context, the document did not require to be probative, the judge expressed the view that this defect could probably have been curable by section 39 procedure.

In the case of a testator who was unable to write, for whatever reason, temporary or permanent, there was a procedure known as notarial execution whereby the document could be signed on the testator's behalf by a solicitor, notary public or parish minister of the Church of Scotland. If the vicarious subscriber had any interest in the will, however fair and above board, this was fatal and the subscription—and thus the entire will—was invalid.

Holograph will

At Scottish common law, a will was regarded as valid if it was written and signed by the testator. The term "holograph" simply means that it is entirely in handwriting. Such a will is not regarded as probative; rather it was said to be "privileged". This means that it can be given the status of probativity if the writing and signature can be proved to be that of the testator. Proof is by way of two affidavits. In practice, the courts have accepted some very informal testamentary writings and, in context, even signatures in "pet" names, e.g. "Connie" (*Draper v Thomson*, 1954 S.C. 136) or "Mum" (*Rhodes v Peterson*, 1972 S.L.T. 98). In practice, if the will is in the testator's writing, it need only be signed on the last page. Once the holograph will is supported by the two affidavits, it is, to all intents and purposes, probative.

It was also perfectly competent (and used to be in virtually universal use among solicitors when submitting offers for heritable property) to adopt a document, written, typed, word processed, printed or a mixture, as holograph of the subscriber. If the subscriber had written the words "adopted as holograph" above the signature, it signified that he regarded the entire document as the equivalent of his own handwriting.

Thus, it is perfectly valid, under the old law, for a testator to adopt a will typed by himself or written or typed by another party. Such a will, even though there are no witnesses, is perfectly valid. There would still be the evidential requirement of two affidavits that the handwriting of the adoption and the signature are those of the testator. What, generally speaking, was insufficient under the old law, was a typed will with a simple signature and without either adoption or the attestation of two witnesses. In *Chisholm v Chisholm*, 1949 S.C. 434, a typed will was signed by the testator without either adoption or attestation. It was not a valid will. There was one maverick case of *McBeath's Trs v McBeath*, 1935 S.C. 471, where the testator typed a will himself and also typed the words "accepted as holograph" above his usual signature. The will contained a statement that it had been typed by the testator. In fact, the testator had a physical disability and it was accepted in court that typing was his normal mode of writing. Accordingly, in the very particular and unusual facts and circumstances of the case, the will was accepted by the court as being holograph of the testator.

Normally, however, the courts would not be so lenient under the old law and the more recent case of *Williamson v Williamson* (above) demonstrates this amply.

It is possible to buy will forms from stationers with certain words already pre-printed, frequently in a "tombstone gothic" type face. The testator fills in the blanks, in relation to legacies, appointment of executor and suchlike. One of the most common problems, particularly under the old law, was that many of these forms were designed for English law, although there are Scottish versions available. Lawyers, of course, do not like them. Certainly, in the wrong hands they can be dangerous weapons.

If, under the old law, such a form was properly signed and witnessed, then the fact that it is partly written and partly printed does not create any problem in itself. The real problem arises where a will form, signed under the old law, was neither adopted nor attested. It would be possible to regard the parts written in the testator's own handwriting as a holograph will in themselves, provided—when read separately—the words could make testamentary sense. In the case of *Macdonald v Cuthbertson* (1890) 18 R. 101, a testator made an unwitnessed will on a printed will form. Reading the printed and handwritten parts together, the will made perfect sense—but there was no way in which the handwritten parts on their own made any sense, testamentary or otherwise. The will was invalid. In the later case of *Carmichael's Exrs v Carmichael*, 1909 S.C. 1387, all the vital words were holograph and it was possible to deduce intelligible intentions from them.

Wills executed on or after August 1, 1995

The Requirements of Writing (Scotland) Act 1995 came into force on August 1, 1995 but only affects documents or deeds executed after it came into force. If a document is undated, it is treated as having been executed under the new law. The changes as they affect the execution of a will are not particularly radical. Verbal nuncupative legacies of moveables not exceeding £8.33 (£100 Scots) disappeared, although, in practice, they had long since gone without trace. The privileged status of a holograph will also disappeared. As explained below, there is no longer any reason for retaining its status.

The basis of the new law is that any document is formally valid if it is subscribed by the granter. This applies to a will as much as to any other legal document. Thus, it does not matter whether the will is handwritten, typed, printed, word processed or a mixture of the above: provided the will is signed at the end, it is formally valid. This is a fail-safe provision which is greatly to be welcomed.

Signatures can include marks and "pet" names, but not if the execution is witnessed. Such signature would require to be fortified by evidence that it was the granter's usual manner of signing or that it was intended, in context, as a signature.

However, there is a further hurdle which must be crossed. If a will is to be used as the basis of confirmation, it requires to be self proving. This is more or less the equivalent of probative under the old law. In other words, if there is any challenge to the execution of the document, the court will presume it to be genuine until the opposite is proved. For a will to have this status, it should be signed on every sheet (which, in practice, is taken to mean every page—and this provision only applies to wills) and the signature should be attested by one witness.

If a will is produced after the testator's death but is not self proving, provided it has been signed (even if only on the last page) it is formally valid, as explained above. By this time it is too late to have it signed on every sheet and witnessed. However, all is not lost. Application can be made to the sheriff for the will to be given self proving status. Evidence that the signature was that of the deceased would be given by affidavit of two appropriate persons.

If the *Williamson* will, referred to above, had been executed under the new law, it would have fared much better. Even if an attestation is botched, the will can still stand as formally valid. It can then be given self proving status, after the necessary proof.

Vicarious subscription

Obviously, there are times when someone wishes to sign a will, but for some reason is unable to write. This might be due to blindness or physical incapacity, temporary or permanent. In such cases, someone else is required to subscribe vicariously. Under the old law, as indicated above, this was achieved by a process known as notarial execution. This meant, in practice, that a will could be signed by a solicitor, provided he had no interest in the will, or by a parish minister of the Church of Scotland. The actual procedure, which involved a docket being handwritten on to the document before two witnesses, had to be meticulously observed to the letter, otherwise the entire will could be void. The more specialised textbooks will take the reader relentlessly through the many pitfalls that existed in this area, should this be required.

Under the new law, vicarious subscription is made somewhat more user-friendly. A "relevant person" may undertake the vicarious subscription, i.e. a practising solicitor, advocate, justice of the peace or sheriff clerk. In theory, a blind person can still sign a deed if he wishes, but that would be highly inadvisable.

The document should be read over to the granter. If the granter wishes to waive the reading he can do so, but this fact should be declared in the testing clause. There is no separate handwritten docket as there was with notarial execution. If the document is a will and it is wished (as it will be) to make it self proving, it should be vicariously subscribed on every page. The witness must see the granter give authority to subscribe and either hear the document being read in full or hear the granter dispense with the reading. The "relevant person" should have no interest in the deed. If it confers a money benefit directly or indirectly on the relevant person, his spouse or child(ren), that particular benefit—but not the entire document—is invalid.

WAS THERE AN INTENTION TO TEST?

Occasionally, a problem may arise in knowing whether a document is actually a will or merely an instruction to another party to draw up a will, or even just a statement of future intention. Crucially, the document would have to pass the tests of formal validity, outlined above, before the court could declare it to be a will. The court would have to be satisfied that there was testamentary intention, but does not look for any particular form of language. Thus in *Rhodes v Peterson* (above), a mother's letter to her daughter was, in context, a will.

If the document is headed "draft" or "rough", as in *Sprot's Trs v Sprot*, 1909 S.C. 272, it will not be counted as a will. The courts have traditionally been less exacting in their standards when considering holograph or home-made wills. A document which appears to express testamentary intention or which gives instructions to a person other than a law agent is much more likely to be accepted as a will than an instruction to a law agent. In *Ayrshire Hospice, Petrs*, 1993 S.L.T. (Sh. Ct) 75, a lady had written a three page document in her own handwriting. It contained a list of legacies to relatives, prefixed by the word "To". The final page referred to "remainder" and gave a list of charities. The document was found in an envelope on which were printed the words "Will of ( )". In context, this was a valid will. Conversely, in the old case of *Munro v Coutts* (1813) 1 Dow 437, a testator sent a letter to his law agent enclosing an apparently valid holograph provision with an instruction to engross it as a codicil. This was held to be no more than an instruction and not a testamentary document.

EXAMPLES OF WILLS

1. The first document is handwritten as follows:

26 Elm Way
Grimburgh
August 10, 1994

Dear Jim,
    As you are my only brother and I have no husband or children of my own, I am relying on you to see that my affairs are properly sorted out after I've gone.
    I would like you to have my house and the furniture as well, apart from the painting of the Town Hall, which I would like you to give to the local museum.
    As for the rest of my stuff—my savings in the bank, my shares and so on—you can divide it up among your girls.
    By the way, Jim, I don't want that wife of yours to get her hands on anything of mine.
    Anyway, Jim, thanks so much for being a good brother.
    Your ever loving and devoted sister
    Beenie

Questions to consider
As it stands is this a valid will?
Have you any particular comments to make about its contents?
Would it make any difference if the date of the letter was August 10, 1995?
What if it was undated?

Comments
Whilst it is not a masterpiece of draughtsmanship, the above is almost certainly a valid will. It is written, signed and clearly has a testamentary intention. It is a holograph will, which requires affidavit evidence that it is in the handwriting of the deceased. Jim appears to be appointed as executor nominate, although more by implication than by express appointment. In a will, for reasons which will be explained in Chapter 11, it is better to avoid words such as "like" and go for stronger verbs such as "instruct" or "direct". Her "stuff" is not adequately described, neither is it clear who Jim's "girls" are. If one daughter were to predecease, did she wish her share to be added on to that of the others or would it fall into intestacy? The gratuitous comment about Jim's wife would have been better left unsaid. As she is not a beneficiary, she will not inherit directly.

If the letter had been signed under the present law, it would be formally valid as it is subscribed by the granter, but there would require to be evidence led that "Beenie" was actually her signature. If the will had been undated, it would be presumed to be executed under the present law.

2. The second will is typewritten and signed:

I, ALBERT ALEXANDER HIGGINS, residing at Eleven Railway Cuttings, Coalburgh, in order to settle my affairs after my death, do hereby leave and bequeath all my means and estate, heritable and moveable, real and personal, wheresoever situated to my wife LETITIA HIGGINS, residing with me at Eleven Railway Cuttings aforesaid; and I appoint my said wife to be my executrix.

Albert A Higgins
August 28, 1994

Questions to consider
As it stands, is this a valid will?
Would it make any difference if it were dated a year later, in 1995?
What if it was undated?

Comments
Unfortunately, it is not a valid will, although it is perfectly clear. It was signed under the old law and, to be valid, it should have been attested or holograph or adopted as holograph. As it is none of these, it is not valid. If it was signed under the present law, or if it was undated, it would be formally valid, although affidavit evidence to fortify the signature would be required in any application for it to be given self proving status.

3. The third will is also typewritten:

I, JON SMYTH, residing at Six Union Square, Aberdeen in order to provide for the succession to my means and estate in the event of my death do hereby leave and bequeath my whole estate both heritable and moveable to my wife DOROTHY, residing with me at Six Union Square aforesaid provided that she survive me by thirty clear days; declaring that in the event of my wife predeceasing me or failing to survive me by thirty clear days I leave and bequeath my said estate equally between my children ALFRED and JOHN; and I declare that it is my wish to be buried with my parents and grandparents in Nellfield Cemetery; And I revoke my former testamentary writings: IN WITNESS WHEREOF I have subscribed these presents at Aberdeen on the Fifth day of August Nineteen Hundred and Ninety Four before these witnesses, Charles Cooper and Jean Donald, both clerks in the employment of Messrs Robb and Steele, Advocates in Aberdeen.

C. Cooper	Witness	*J Smyth*
John Donald	Witness	

Question to consider
Is the above will valid?

Comments
The will looks all right at first glance but, on a closer inspection, there is something wrong with the attestation. The testing clause names "Jean Donald" as a witness whereas the signature is clearly "John Donald". Assuming that all the parties have signed their correct names, the will is not probative because, under the old law, two correctly identified witnesses required to sign. However, an error of this type in a testing clause could be counted as an informality of execution, curable by section 39 procedure. This is different from the *Williamson* case where one of the witnesses failed to sign his correct name.

---

6. COMMON TESTAMENTARY PROVISIONS

The law generally presumes in favour of a testator's freedom. Even in today's complex and highly regulated society, people may generally do as they please with their own property when alive. Similarly, they can decide how to dispose of it after death. As demonstrated in Chapter 3, the important exception to this proposition is found in legal rights since they can never be defeated by a will.

However, there can be cases where conditions attached to a legacy are seen as being objectionable and so are not given effect.

VOID CONDITIONS

Impossibility, illegality, immorality or provisions contrary to public policy
A condition may be void if it is impossible, illegal, immoral or contrary to public policy, e.g. that the beneficiary is to marry the

testator's daughter, otherwise he does not get the legacy. The void condition, in such a case, is said to be *pro non scripto* (as not having been written), but the actual legacy does not fall, merely the objectionable condition. One of the obvious difficulties is knowing what, in today's diverse society, counts as immoral. What is contrary to public policy may be even more elusive. In *Fraser v Rose* (1849) 11 D. 1466, a daughter was left a legacy by her father on condition that she did not live with her mother (the deceased's widow) who was to be thrown out of the house. The court set aside the condition and the daughter received the legacy unconditionally. Similarly, in the English case of *Re Johnson's Will Trusts* [1967] 1 All E.R. 553, a condition attached to a legacy which could be seen as an encouragement to a wife to leave her spouse was declared to be ineffectual. On the other hand, in *Earl of Caithness v Sinclair*, 1912 S.C. 79, it was not contrary to public policy to make a legacy conditional on the beneficiary not succeeding to a peerage.

Sometimes there is no identifiable beneficiary and, in this case, if the conditions are "objectionable", the entire legacy will fall. Some eccentric testators have attempted to do some rather remarkable things. In *McCaig v University of Glasgow*, 1907 S.C. 231, Mr McCaig, who built the famous "folly" overlooking Oban, directed his testamentary trustees to erect artistic towers and statues of himself and his family on his estate. His sister challenged the legacy and the court struck it down as being of no benefit to anyone. As if that were not enough, some years later, the same sister attempted to do something similar in her will, which included erecting statues of the McCaig family on top of the "folly". In *McCaig's Trs v Lismore United Free Kirk Session*, 1915 S.C. 426, the provisions were struck down and, as there was no beneficiary, the legacy could not be paid. In *Aitken's Trs v Aitken*, 1927 S.C. 374, a Musselburgh butcher directed that his shop was to be demolished and, on its site, was to be erected a massive bronze equestrian statue of himself in his uniform of Champion of the Riding of the Marches. Again, this legacy was struck down. To put it in non-legal language, the provision was "over the top". Expressed more conventionally, such provisions have been seen by the court as an abuse of the power of testation.

In *Mackintosh's J.F. v Lord Advocate*, 1935 S.C. 406, a lady who was illegitimate by birth directed that her entire estate was to be spent on erecting a mausoleum in which her remains were to be interred, along with those of two predeceasing friends, whose remains would first have had to exhumed. Whilst there is no objection to providing a reasonable memorial for oneself, this provision was grotesque. It might possibly have been different if the two friends had been close members of the family. There is a sad element in this case. Perhaps the testator was trying to create a proper family for herself after her death at a time when popular views on illegitimacy were different from the present day. As stated earlier, the 2006 Act finally removed the status of illegitimacy.

In *Sutherland's Tr. v Verschoyle*, 1968 S.L.T. 43, a lady made provision in her will to preserve and display her art collection. In fact, the collection was not of outstanding value and was, in any case, somewhat of a mixture. The court took the view that to provide for the display of such an unimportant collection would be so wasteful as to be contrary to public policy.

The matter of a legacy failing because of uncertainty is considered further in Chapter 11.

Repugnancy

A legacy is said to have a repugnant condition if that condition is inconsistent with the main tenor of the legacy itself. One example would be where a legacy appears to be given absolutely and without restriction, but trustees are then directed to hold the capital and pay only the revenue to the beneficiary. In such a case, the direction to the trustees to hold the capital would be repugnant and the beneficiary would receive payment of the capital of his legacy. Another possible example would be where a testator directs that an annuity be purchased for the legatee, as in *Dow v Kilgour's Trs* (1877) 4 R. 403, but the legatee could immediately sell the annuity for a lump sum. In such a case, the beneficiary would be entitled to payment of the lump sum which would have been used to buy the annuity. In *Miller's Trs v Miller* (1890) 18 R. 301, a father left property in trust for his son. The trustees of the estate were directed to administer the property until he attained the age of 25, or on his earlier marriage, at which date he would attain a full vested right. The son married before the age of 25 but his father's trustees refused to denude in his favour. It was held that where an absolute right of property is given to a beneficiary of full age, he can require the trustees to denude in his favour, even if the original will had directed retention for a longer period. If there had been other trust purposes still to be carried out, or if the trustees had been given some element of discretion, the son would not have been able to make the trustees denude until he attained the age of 25.

Accumulation of income

Although now contained in later statute, the law originated in the Accumulations Act 1800, better known as the Thelluson Act. In *Thelluson v Woodford* (1799) 4 Ves. 227; (1805) 11 Ves. 112, a very wealthy English merchant directed that his entire estate was to be invested in land and the income accumulated. His estate was only to be shared out among members of his family when the last of the class of his children and/or grandchildren died. In other words, he was effectively passing over two generations. In Scotland, his children could at least have claimed legal rights but not so south of the border. When the case came to the House of Lords, it was decided, with reluctance, that the provisions of the will were valid. The 1800 Act was passed as a knee-jerk reaction to ensure that history did not repeat itself. The current law is found in the Trusts (Scotland) Act 1961 and the Law Reform (Miscellaneous Provisions) (Scotland) Act 1966, although they are still referred to as the Thelluson Act provisions. It is not possible to contract out of these statutory provisions. There are actually six possible maximum periods of accumulation, explained in the more detailed and specialised textbooks.

As far as testamentary trustees are concerned, the simple rule of thumb is that income cannot be accumulated for more than 21 years from the death of the testator. Income directed to be accumulated contrary to the statutory provisions goes to those who would have otherwise been entitled to it, i.e. if accumulation had not been directed in the first place. It is perfectly legal to accumulate for up to 21 years—and whatever fund is thus "in the bag" is perfectly legitimate—but after the 21 years have passed, the surplus income must be distributed even if the original will or trust disposition and settlement provide otherwise.

One leading case is *Elder's Trs v Free Church of Scotland* (1892) 20 R. 2. Mr Elder provided in his will for an adequate annuity for his widow, but the whole residue of his estate was to be held by trustees until her death. On Mrs Elder's death, the trustees were to set aside certain legacies to provide a Chair in one of the Free Church Colleges, to erect and endow a new Free Church, with a manse, and to apply any remaining estate to schemes of the Free Church to be selected by his trustees. The income from the estate more than covered Mrs Elder's annuity and surplus income was accumulated. She survived her husband by more than 21 years, so further accumulation thereafter was void. The question arose as to who was entitled to this surplus revenue. Not surprisingly, the Free Church of Scotland claimed to be the residuary legatee and thus entitled to the revenue. However, the Church was not the residuary legatee. The residue was to be paid to schemes of the Church to be selected by the trustees and this selection could only take place after Mrs Elder died. So, until Mrs Elder died, there could be no residuary legatee. Accordingly, the surplus revenue fell into intestate succession.

It is not possible, however, for legal rights to be claimed out of such revenue as it has come into the estate after the death of the testator, as was demonstrated in the case of *Lindsay's Trs v Lindsay*, 1931 S.C. 586.

Creation of certain liferents
The Law Reform (Miscellaneous Provisions) (Scotland) Act 1968 section 18 provides that it is not possible to create a liferent (explained more fully below) in favour of someone who is not alive or *in utero* (in the womb) at the date of the creator's death. If someone tries to do this, the effect is that the liferent property belongs absolutely to the beneficiary at the date when he becomes entitled to the liferent, provided he is aged 18. If the beneficiary is younger, he must wait until attaining the age of 18.

COMMON PROVISIONS IN A WILL

Most testators are not too concerned about what they cannot do by will. They want to achieve something much more positive and to provide a fair and just settlement of their affairs after their death. In practice, many testators make quite simple wills, perhaps leaving all property to a spouse, or to a spouse and children, or to close relatives or even a favourite charity. In other cases, the testator may wish to make more detailed provisions by way of (1) legacy, (2) annuity or (3) liferent. These will now be examined in turn.

LEGACIES

Legacies can be divided into three main categories: special, general or residuary. A special (or specific) legacy is, as the name would suggest, a bequest of a specific item such as a house, a grandfather clock or "my shares in Black & White plc".

A general legacy is one in which the subject matter of the item has no distinct individual character of its own to distinguish it from others of the same kind. The easiest and most common example is a sum of money, e.g. "the sum of £5,000". It could also be a quantity of goods coming under a generic or general description.

The residue of the estate is whatever is left after the special and general legacies are paid in full. Obviously, the amount of residue will vary greatly, depending on what is included in the estate. A residuary legatee could receive nothing or next to nothing—or could receive a very large amount. In many cases, it falls somewhere in between. These categories are not merely artificial. The executor must pay the legacies in the order of special first, followed secondly by general and lastly the residue.

Abatement

A problem can arise when, even although the estate is solvent (i.e. all debts can be paid), there is not enough left to pay every beneficiary in full. This problem is dealt with by bringing in certain presumptions, unless the will expressly provides otherwise. These presumptions are known as the rules on abatement (cutting back).

Specific legacies must be paid first and in full, even if there is not sufficient to pay general legatees in full. Thus a specific legatee, in many ways, is in the best position.

General legacies are paid next. If there is not sufficient to pay them in full, they are abated *pari passu* (in equal proportion). Thus, you might have a legacy to John of £2,000 and a legacy of £1,000 to Jean, but there is only £1,500 available. In such a case, both legacies would suffer a 50 per cent abatement, giving John £1,000 and Jean £500.

Lastly, the residue is paid over. If there is nothing left, the residuary legatee gets nothing. To put this another way, the residue is the first class of legacies to be abated, even although, in practice, it is last to be paid. A practical example may be helpful:

George has died, leaving the following net estate, all moveable:

Grandfather clock	£750
Bureau	£2,000
Other effects	£5,000
Shares	£10,000
Bank balance	£15,000

In his will, he made the following provisions:

John	grandfather clock
Mabel	bureau
Alan	£12,000
Bill	£4,000
Joan	£8,000
Mavis	£8,000
Nigel	residue

John and Mabel are in the best position because their legacies, being special, are paid first and in full. The remaining moveable property is valued at £30,000 and must be applied towards the payment of the general legacies. If the legacies were to be paid in full, this would require a sum of £32,000. Thus the legacies require to be abated in the ratio of 30/32. This means that Alan receives £11,250, Bill £3,750 and Joan and Mavis each £7,500. Nigel, the residuary legatee, sees his legacy being abated in full and he gets nothing.

Ademption of special legacies

Where a testator provides for a special legacy and, at the date of his death, the subject of the legacy no longer forms part of his estate, the legacy is said to be adeemed (the noun is ademption) and nothing is due to the legatee. The motives of the testator in disposing of the item are irrelevant. Thus if Uncle Fred leaves the grandfather clock to nephew David but, at the date of his death, he no longer owns the clock, David's legacy lapses and nothing is due to him under this heading.

Legatum rei alienae

Occasionally, a testator may leave something in his will which never belonged to him (as distinct from an article which did once belong to him but of which he has disposed). This is obviously different from ademption and is known as *legatum rei alienae* (legacy of a thing belonging to someone else). The normal presumption is that the testator made a mistake and, accordingly, the legacy fails. However, if it can be proved that the testator knew that the property was not his, then the legacy can be interpreted as an instruction to buy the item from its owner or, if it cannot be bought, to hand over the value to the legatee. Fairly obviously, it may be difficult, if not impossible, to prove what the testator knew.

ANNUITIES

An annuity is the right to a periodical fixed payment of a sum of money from the revenue of the estate. It can also be used to signify an arrangement with a financial institution in which, in return for a capital sum, an income is paid, usually for the remainder of a person's life. At this stage, we are confining ourselves to the first alternative. An annuity may be created in favour of any person either *inter vivos* (taking effect during the lifetime of the granter) or *mortis causa* (by will). The annuity may be for any sum that the granter wishes and may continue as long as he desires. The most common practice is to provide an annuity for a beneficiary for his or her lifetime but it should be noted that the granter may fix the period for a shorter time. There may even be a provision that the annuity will terminate should some particular event take place, such as the re-marriage of the beneficiary. On the other hand, an annuity, unlike a liferent (below), need not be limited to the lifetime of a human being. It could be granted for a longer period or it could even be perpetual, such as the endowment of a prize fund. Nowadays, such an endowment would more likely be provided by an initial capital sum which trustees would invest and use the fluctuating interest to fund the particular purpose.

Assuming that the annuity is granted *mortis causa* the testator can fix the method by which it is to be paid. However, if he directs that an annuity is to be bought for the beneficiary by way of a lump sum payment to an insurance company, with the result that the beneficiary could sell the annuity in return for a capital sum, this could be an example of a repugnant condition (explained above). Normally the testator will provide that the annuitant is entitled to an annuity of £X *per annum* out of the free annual income of the estate. This means that the payment of the annuity is made without diminishing the capital of the estate. However, if, in the future, the income of the trust funds is not sufficient to pay the annuity in full, the trustees must make up the full amount of the annuity by encroaching on the capital (unless the trust deed prohibits this, in which case the annuity would have to be reduced).

Although traditionally an annuity was for a fixed sum, the value of such an income is bound to be eroded by inflation. It is perfectly in order for an annuity provision to be inflation-proofed in some way, but this has to be provided for expressly, not merely by implication.

LIFERENT AND FEE

It is necessary to distinguish a liferent from an annuity. It has just been demonstrated that, unless provided to the contrary, trustees may encroach on capital (if need be) to pay an annuity in full. The opposite rule applies to a liferent, as (unless the will provides otherwise) no encroachment on capital is permitted. Although liferent can be provided *inter vivos* it is more commonly provided *mortis causa*. A key element of liferent is that there must always be a right of fee, i.e. a full and unencumbered right of property, at the end of the liferent period. So, a common enough provision would be ". . . to my wife Doris in liferent and my son John in fee". If what purports to be a liferent does not have a right of fee at its conclusion, whatever else it may be, it is not a liferent.

The liferenter has the right to use the property and enjoy the income and fruits from it *salva substantia* (without destruction of the substance). It is sometimes necessary to make a fine distinction between income and capital. In the case of an estate of timber, the rule appears to be that the liferenter is entitled to ordinary windfalls, to copse-wood cut in normal course and to wood cut for estate purposes such as fencing. The fiar (person entitled to the fee) is entitled to final mature trees and to trees blown down by extraordinary storms. The liferenter is entitled to royalties from mineral workings let or worked during the lifetime of the testator.

Royalties from minerals let or worked after the testator's death normally fall into capital. The liferenter is entitled to dividends from shares and to other cash payments made by the company out of profits. Bonus shares are classed as capital unless they are issued in lieu of a cash dividend. Most liferents set up by a will are said to be "beneficiary" (sometimes called "improper") which means that the property is held by trustees during the liferent period. At the end of the liferent, the trustees denude in favour of the fiar.

The Apportionment Act 1870 provides that all rents, regular annual receipts, dividends and interest are to be considered as accruing from day to day. This means in practice that the liferenter is only entitled to income on the trust investments which actually accrue during the liferent period. So, income accrued before the commencement of the liferent period (usually the date of the testator's death) falls ("effeirs") to capital, as does income accrued after its termination. If shares are bought during the liferent, the liferenter receives only the proportion of dividend accrued after purchase. Similarly, if shares are sold, the liferenter only receives the proportion of income accrued up to date of sale. Clearly, this is all rather complicated. It is perfectly competent, and invariable professional practice, to disapply the provisions of the Act in the testamentary deed.

The crucial concept to grasp is that the fiar actually owns the property but cannot enjoy the fee absolute (ownership *and* possession) until the burden of the liferent comes to an end.

Traditionally, liferents tended to affect heritable property but, with the passage of time, liferents of both heritable and moveable property have become more common. A classic situation would be where a testator directs that his house is to be held by his trustees in liferent to his widow until her death or remarriage and then to the child(ren) in fee. The effect of this provision is that the widow may continue to live in the house without it ever becoming her property.

One obvious good reason for such a provision is to prevent the house going out of the family, should the liferenter remarry. Although a fiar does acquire a vested right in the property at the time of the testator's death (*a morte testatoris*), actual possession of the subjects is not given until the termination of the liferent. To put it another way, the widow's liferent is a burden on the fiar's right to the property so that although the fiar could sell the property during the subsistence of the liferent, he cannot give a higher or better right than he himself possesses. Thus any purchaser or secured creditor can only take the property subject to the rights of the liferenter.

There is no reason for a liferent to be gender specific although, traditionally, more liferents have been enjoyed by women than men.

As indicated above, liferent includes the rights to enjoy the fruits or income from property without diminishing the capital. So if (as is often the case) the liferented property is a house, the liferenter (to use the example quoted above) would bear the expense of the upkeep of the property, plus the usual burdens such as local taxes, insurance and normal maintenance (an elusive concept at the best of times) of the property. The liferenter would also pay any interest on a heritable security, but would not be liable to repay any of the capital of an outstanding mortgage. Larger repairs or more fundamental alterations or renovations would probably be the responsibility of the fiar but each instance would have to be considered on its merits. In practice, parties may come to their own arrangements about who pays for what.

If the liferenter were to leave the property for good, it would revert to the fiar in fee absolute.

Alimentary liferents
Sometimes a liferent is declared in the will to be alimentary, with the intention of providing for the maintenance of the liferenter. Traditionally, a liferent was declared to be alimentary in order to provide the liferenter with some safeguard against personal rashness and to give some protection against hard times. It would be of most relevance where the property includes more than a dwelling house, such as an element of income.

The two main features and advantages of an alimentary liferent are:

(1) It may not be assigned, e.g. by sale, gift or security, to a third party. The alimentary liferent is entirely personal to the liferenter. Once it has been accepted, it cannot be assigned or renounced.

(2) It is not liable to the diligence of creditors. This means that the liferent funds may not be arrested in the hands of the trustees, as third parties. It should, however, be noted that it is only protected to the extent that the income payable to the liferenter is reasonable, bearing in mind the liferenter's own personal circumstances and position in life. Any excess over such a reasonable amount will be liable to diligence. What is reasonable is always a matter of fact.

Of course, not everyone who receives an alimentary liferent is foolish or wayward in financial matters!

There are cases where a beneficiary has wished to assign or renounce the liferent. At common law, an alimentary liferent cannot be revoked once it has become operational. It can, however, be revoked *before* it becomes operational (*Douglas-Hamilton v Duke and Duchess of Hamilton's Trs*, 1961 S.C. 205). Under section 1 of the Trusts (Scotland) Act 1961, the court may allow an arrangement to vary or revoke an alimentary liferent provided it is satisfied that such an arrangement is reasonable in the circumstances, e.g. that there is sufficient income from other sources for the maintenance of the liferenter. Normally an alimentary liferent is expressly declared by the testator to be alimentary, but this is not actually essential. Provided the testator makes it clear in some other words that the liferent is of an alimentary nature, this is sufficient in law to give it that status.

Right of occupancy
It is necessary to distinguish a right of liferent from a right of occupancy of a dwellinghouse. The latter right is a lesser right than that of liferent; it merely confers a personal right to occupy the subjects stated for a specific period, as directed. An occupant would be liable for local taxes, but not for the type of repairs normally carried out by a landlord nor for interest on a heritable security. Sometimes there may be a problem in deciding whether the testator has, in fact, granted a right of occupancy or a liferent. In the case of *Cathcart's Trs v Allardice* (1899) 2 F. 326, it was held that even though the word "liferent" had been used in a will, only a right to occupy had been intended.

---

7. RESIDUARY AND SUBSTITUTIONARY PROVISIONS

In the course of human history, many people have claimed to be able to see into the future. Readers can make their own assessments of such claims. However, in dealing with succession, it is not necessary to attempt to foretell the future—but it is necessary to consider at least a range of viable possibilities as to what eventualities could take place in the future.

Once a potential testator has decided in principle what he wishes to be done with his estate after death, the obvious next step should be to consult with his solicitor so that an appropriate will can be drawn up and signed. It is not surprising that some parts of a professionally drafted will are in formal legal jargon but most simple modern wills are perfectly easy for a lay person to understand. The language of a will is intended to avoid confusion, not to create it.

THE RESIDUE CLAUSE

It is fair to assume that if a person makes a will, the intention is that this document will deal with the whole of his estate. It would be both perverse and unwise to want to leave a will which only disposes of part of the estate and leaves the rest to intestate succession. In Chapter 4 it was shown how a partial intestacy might arise, but few people, if any, would purposely set out to achieve such an inconvenient mess being made of their affairs after their death.

Very few people know exactly how much they are worth in purely financial terms. There is an uncomfortable ring of truth in the cynical saying that most people are "better off dead". Even if a person knows roughly what his house and furniture is worth and how much he has in the bank or building society, it is unlikely that he will be able to take account of every last penny which will be credited to his estate.

One of the many problems of the home-made will is that, surprisingly often, a testator will forget altogether about the residue of his estate. He will make bequests of his house and valuables and general legacies to a number of people—but forget about all that is left over. If there has been a long interval between making the will and his actual death, that residue could have increased very substantially. Equally, it could also have diminished, if the testator was living on capital.

A typical example of a residue clause would be "I leave the rest, residue and remainder of my means and estate to. . ." It is common enough, and perfectly in order, for a residuary legatee to be given a special or general legacy in addition, e.g. he may receive the grandfather clock and the residue or a share of the residue. The rules of abatement and ademption of specific legacies, explained in Chapter 6, would apply.

THE DESTINATION-OVER

A major purpose of a residue clause is to prevent any part of the estate falling into intestacy. Of course, a problem could arise if the residuary legatee were to die before the testator. The general rule, already explored, is that no one can benefit under a will unless he survives the testator. This might seem almost painfully obvious, since how can anyone benefit if he is dead? That is fair comment, but the question does not so much concern a benefit which the predeceasing legatee did not have the opportunity to enjoy—the real question is, did he, at the time of his death, have what is called a vested right? If he did, that vested right can pass on to his heirs. It is crucially important to understand that a potential beneficiary cannot have a vested right if he dies before the testator. The wider issue of vesting is explored in Chapter 8.

One way of avoiding the residue—or indeed any kind of legacy—failing altogether, is to have at least one alternative legatee "up one's sleeve". This can be achieved by a "whom failing provision", e.g. the legacy goes ". . . to John, whom failing Betty". The technical name for a "whom failing" provision is a "destination-over". Such a device is simple to insert and common in practice. If John dies before the testator, he has no vested right and the legacy will pass to Betty (assuming, of course, that she does survive the testator).

However, there is another potential problem. Suppose that at the time of the testator's death, John is alive. Obviously, the legacy vests in him. So, where does that leave Betty? Does she have any hope of eventually succeeding to that same legacy when John dies? The simple answer is usually not, but the matter requires further exploration. Unfortunately, it is necessary to look at some technical jargon at this point.

In the destination-over, John is the institute, i.e. the main legatee. Betty, on the other hand, is either the conditional institute or the substitute. If she is the conditional institute, the position is clear. When John inherits the legacy, Betty's right is said to "fly off". This is a curiously colloquial expression but abundantly clear in its meaning.

If, however, Betty is the substitute there is just a possibility that she could still inherit after John's death. It all depends on what John does during the time of his ownership. If he alienates the legacy by sale or gift or if he leaves it in his will to someone other than Betty, any right she might have had in it is effectively defeated. But if he does not take any such steps, she could claim it on his death.

Obviously, the crucial opening question is whether Betty is a conditional institute or a substitute. The first place to look is the actual will itself in the hope that the testator's intentions are clear. If the will is unclear, or is silent, certain legal presumptions will be invoked. If the subject of the legacy is heritable, Betty will be a substitute. If it is moveable, she is merely a conditional institute. In

Crumpton's J.F. v Barnardo's Homes, 1917 S.C. 713, money was left to certain charities in case the original legatee (institute) were to die without issue. In fact, the institute did die without leaving issue but, because the will was silent on the matter and because the legacy was of moveables, the charities were conditional institutes. Their potential right had flown off when the institute inherited. By contrast, in *Watson v Giffen* (1884) 11 R. 444, a lady bequeathed heritable property (a half-share of the family home) to her son, whom failing her brother. The son inherited the half-share but died intestate and still in ownership of it. Because heritable property was involved and the will was silent, the brother was the substitute and inherited. Significantly, he did not inherit moveable property passing under the same will on similar terms. This illustrates that the legal presumptions in this area appear to be strong. The counsel of perfection for anyone drawing up a will containing a destination-over is to ensure that it does actually contain the full wishes of the deceased.

If, to return to the fictitious example above, John dies before the testator, Betty simply inherits the property. The question as to whether she is a conditional institute or a substitute would be academic.

---

8. VESTING AND ACCRETION

VESTING OF LEGACIES

In previous chapters, several references have been made to the concept of vesting. If property vests in someone, it is his property. However, it is quite possible to have a vested right in something but not to have possession or full enjoyment of it for a variety of different reasons. A person who is in employment has a vested right to each day of salary which he earns. However, he does not actually receive payment until the appropriate pay day. But should he die during the pay period (say, in the middle of the month), the portion of accrued salary will have vested and would be payable to his estate.

It is possible, in fact, for someone to have a vested right in something but not to have the full possession and enjoyment for many years to come. Indeed, it is perfectly possible for someone to die with a vested right, never having enjoyed possession at all. Nevertheless, the question as to whether a right has vested is not merely academic; it is crucial in the matter of succession. It should be obvious that, in a common calamity (see Chapter 2), it could be of the utmost importance to know or presume the order of death, even if that is (mistakenly) perceived by members of the family as macabre and insensitive.

It is necessary to start with the basics. Until a testator dies, there can be no vested right for a beneficiary. The most the beneficiary can enjoy during the testator's lifetime are expectations. The problem with expectations is that they can be dashed. Thus even if Aunt Flossie names her nephew Herbert as her sole beneficiary, and even if she delivers the will into his hands, he has no vested right. He might die before her, or she could change her mind and execute another will, revoking the one in Herbert's possession. Delivery of a will, even to a beneficiary, does not make it irrevocable. Indeed, even if a will states that its provisions are irrevocable, this statement is of no effect and the testator can still change his mind.

It is only on the death of the testator that rights in succession can actually vest. Indeed, to put this another way, it can be stated quite categorically that the earliest date on which a legacy can vest in a beneficiary is the date of the testator's death. Thus, if there is a clear unconditional bequest, whether general, special or residuary, and the legatee is alive at the time of the testator's death, the legacy vests *a morte testatoris* (from the testator's death). If that legatee subsequently dies before taking possession of the legacy, it will, in turn, pass under his will or his intestacy, as the case may be.

It may be that vesting is postponed for one reason or another. The will should make the position clear. If there is doubt, the general presumption is in favour of early vesting.

But why should vesting ever be postponed? It is easier to answer that question by giving examples:

Example 1. ". . . to my nephew John, provided he survives me by thirty clear days . . ."

Example 2. ". . . to my widow Josephine in liferent and to my son Marmaduke in fee . . ."

Looking at the first example, it is a clear condition of the will that John will not acquire any vested right unless and until he survives the testator by 30 clear days. This kind of provision is increasingly common to prevent a double passing of property in quick succession, as was demonstrated in Chapter 2. In this example, the date of vesting is tied to an *uncertain* day. That may sound illogical since such a date can clearly be traced on any calendar by taking the deceased's date of death and adding on 30 days. But, although that date is easily identified, the fact that John will survive for 30 days is not certain. The chances are that he will, but until the uncertainty disappears, there can be no vested right. If he does survive for the 30 days, the uncertainty is removed and on that 30th day he acquires a vested right. This concept is sometimes expressed in the rather grand Latin maxim *dies incertus pro conditione habetur* (an uncertain day is treated as a condition). Even if he was unfortunate enough to die on that day, the legacy would have vested and his heirs would be able to claim it. This tying to an uncertain day is also sometimes known as a suspensive condition, simply because vesting is suspended until the uncertainty is removed.

The second example perhaps brings a more surprising result, if we look at it from the point of view of Marmaduke. His right is tied to a *certain day*, namely a day that sooner or later *must* arrive. It is not possible to plot it on the calendar, but nevertheless it is certain. What is certain in this example? The fact that, sooner or later, the liferent must come to an end. It will end when (not if) one of the following events take place: (1) the liferenter dies or (2) the liferenter renounces the liferent or (3) (if the will expressly provides for this) the liferenter remarries.

Marmaduke's right of fee, accordingly, is tied to a certain day, i.e. the end of the liferent. This means that the fee vests in him on the death of his father. Obviously, he does not have possession, but the fee belongs to him, subject to the burden of the liferent. Thus, he can dispose of his right of fee as he wishes, subject always to the rights of the liferenter, and if he predeceases his mother, his right of fee will vest in his heirs. When, eventually, the liferent ends, Marmaduke will enjoy what is called the fee absolute or fee simple, i.e. the fee without any incumbrance of liferent. However, although he will then have full possession, his ownership does not begin at that point, it merely continues.

Among the more problematic legacies in respect of vesting are those where there is some tie to a beneficiary reaching a particular age. As explained above, this is normally counted as a suspensive condition, thus there can be no vesting until the beneficiary attains the stipulated age. However, it is necessary to read the will very carefully as the above rules are actually no more than presumptions where a will is silent on the matter. There is a crucial difference between a legacy vesting *now* in a young person, but being held on his behalf by trustees until he attains, say, the age of 25, and a legacy which gives a particular benefit *provided* the beneficiary survives to age 25, which suspends vesting until that age is attained.

The whole point about vesting is that it gives an element of security to a beneficiary. All the parties (in theory) are aware of their position. It may now come as a surprise to learn that there are cases when even a vested right may be defeated or, in legal jargon, may be subject to defeasance. This is also known as a resolutive condition in a legacy. Sometime there may not be complete defeasance, in which case it is said to be partial. An easy example would where John leaves property to his wife Jean in liferent and to "our children" in fee. If there are two children at the time of John's death, they take an immediate vested right in the fee, i.e. half of "the cake". Suppose Jean was pregnant with their third child at the time of her husband's death. When that third child is born, he will acquire an immediate vested right to a share in the fee. This means that the right of the other two children is partly defeated. All three children now have a vested right in one third of the fee.

An example of full defeasance would be where Peter leaves his estate in liferent to his widow Sharon and to their as yet unborn child, whom failing his sister Gertrude. On Peter's death, Gertrude takes an immediate vested right in the fee. If Sharon was pregnant at the time of her husband's death and their child is subsequently born, Gertrude's right of fee is fully defeated.

Vesting is a complex subject in its own right. It can often arise in the context of a destination-over. If the testator directs his trustees to pay a legacy on the occurrence of an event (frequently the testator's death) whom failing to another, obviously the original beneficiary does not take any immediate vested right. So, if the original beneficiary dies before the testator, he cannot acquire any vested right (hopefully, this is now self evident) and the destination-over takes effect on the death of the testator.

There are cases where the legacy does not vest until a later (uncertain) date—but the same rules will apply, in that survivorship is essential to the acquiring of a vested right. Thus, even if the institute does survive the testator but dies before the time of vesting, the destination-over will operate on the death of the institute and any right will pass to the conditional institute or substitute (and, at this point, the distinction between the two does not matter).

EXCEPTIONS TO THE SURVIVORSHIP RULE IN VESTING

Having been at great pains to stress the importance of vesting, it is right to point out two exceptions to the general rule about survivorship being of the essence.

(1) The first exception has already been covered under intestate succession and legal rights. One of the more radical changes

brought about by the 1964 Act was the right of children and other direct descendants to represent their parent or ancestor in respect of claims for legitim or against the dead's part. Before 1964, there was no such right. That position was logical, but was perceived as being unfair. It is important to remember that although legal rights can be claimed in spite of the provisions in a will, dead's part cannot, since it literally only applies under intestate succession.

(2) The second exception has a rather long name—the *conditio si institutus sine liberis decesserit* (better known as the *conditio si institutus*). Translated, it means "the condition that the institute shall have died without children". In limited cases, a condition may be read into a bequest that where the institute dies before acquiring a vested right, the institute's children, if they are not provided for in the will, may inherit in preference to other beneficiaries, such as a residuary legatee.

The *conditio si institutus* can only apply where the predeceasing institute is closely related to the testator and is based on the presumption that, if the testator had foreseen that the institute might die before him, he would have wished the institute's children to take in place of their parent. In practice this will only happen when the predeceasing institute is a direct descendant of the testator. It would not include a step-child. In theory, it can also apply if the institute is a nephew or niece but only if the testator has placed himself *in loco parentis* to them, i.e. treated them in the will as a parent would normally do. In practice, the relevance of the *conditio si institutus* to nephews or nieces is slight.

The *conditio* will not apply if the will indicates expressly or by clear implication that the testator did not intend it to. So, if it is clear that a testator made a bequest to a nephew out of personal favour to that individual, rather than mere relationship, the *conditio* would not apply. Also, it would not apply where the testator makes express provision elsewhere in the will for the institute's descendants. This kind of situation could not normally arise unless in the context of litigation or by agreement among the family. It would be a rash executor who would take the law into his own hands and apparently bypass another claimant without the authority of the court or a formal writing from the beneficiaries who would lose by the invocation of the *conditio*.

Although it is nothing to do with the above, this is as good a time as any to mention the *conditio si testator sine liberis decesserit*. Do not confuse the *conditio si testator* with the *conditio si institutus* dealt with above. It used to be a favourite question of examiners to ask what the difference is between the two. That is an artificial question since they are entirely different apart from the fact that they look alike. It is the sort of question which no one, apart from an examiner, ever asks.

The *conditio si testator* is an ancient common law presumption that where a testator makes a universal settlement, e.g. "my whole means and estate to. . .", that will is revoked by the subsequent birth of a child to the testator. The presumption raised by the *conditio* is based on the notion that the testator would not have wished such a will to stand where it made no provision for the child or children. The presumption could be rebutted by circumstances which show that the testator intended that his will should stand in spite of the subsequent birth of the child, e.g. if he made suitable *inter vivos* provisions for the child.

In fact, the *conditio* does not operate automatically. It can only be invoked by a later born child. It is doubtful whether it has any great significance since the passing of the 1964 Act. If a child succeeds in revoking his parent's will by using the *conditio*, that will is totally revoked and the estate will have to be divided according to the rules of intestate succession. If this happens, there is the risk that the entire estate is eaten up by the surviving spouse claiming prior rights. For the child, this is the equivalent of scoring an own goal. A later born child would be better advised to claim legal rights out of the estate. As has been demonstrated more than once in the earlier parts of the book, legal rights cannot be excluded by will, nor does claiming them put the estate into intestacy. The Scottish Law Commission has recommended that the *conditio si testator* be abolished.

PRACTICAL EXAMPLE OF VESTING

The following is a copy of an actual will, drawn from the writer's own family archives.

I, MRS ISABELLA MORTIMER or GORDON residing in South Street, Elgin, Widow of the late John Gordon, Plumber in Elgin, in order to settle my affairs in the event of my death, Do hereby Give, Grant, Assign and Dispone to and in favour of my son George Gordon, my daughter Elsie Gordon and my Brother-in-law, Thomas Forsyth, Flesher in Elgin and the acceptors and acceptor, survivors and survivor of them as Trustees and Trustee for the ends, uses and purposes aftermentioned, my whole means and estate, heritable and moveable, real and personal, wheresoever situated, presently belonging or which shall pertain and belong to me at the time of my death with the writs, vouchers and instructions thereof, and I nominate my said trustees to be my executors, declaring that these presents are granted in trust (First) For payment of all my just and lawful debts, deathbed and funeral expenses and the expenses of this trust; (Second) That my

*trustees shall give the use of the dwellinghouse now occupied by me or
in lieu thereof another dwellinghouse, being part of my heritable
property, together with the household furniture belonging to me, to my
unmarried daughters so long as any of them remain unmarried; and
after payment of the rates, taxes, burdens, necessary repairs and
interest of borrowed money on the heritable property shall divide the
annual proceeds thereof among my daughters Elsie, Isabella, Chris-
tina Jane and Williamina Mortimer and the survivors of them, share
and share alike, and on the death of all my said daughters to realise
the property and divide the proceeds equally share and share alike
among my sons John, George and James, the lawful issue of any of
my said sons predeceasing the term of division taking their parent's
share, the furniture to be divided among my daughters equally on the
whole being married or on the death of the last surviving unmarried
one; (Third) Any other property which I may be possessed of at the
time of my death I direct my trustees after fulfilment of the first head
of this trust to divide among my daughters share and share alike and I
hereby authorise my trustees if they in their discretion consider it
necessary or advisable for carrying out the purposes of this trust, to
sell the whole or any part of the heritable or moveable property or to
borrow money on the security thereof and in the event of a sale I
direct the trustees to invest the trust funds and pay the interest thereof
to my daughters in the manner provided by the Second purpose of this
trust; and I authorise my trustees to appoint one or more of their own
number or others to be factors or agents in the trust and to pay them
suitable remuneration to invest the trust funds on such securities
heritable or moveable as to them may seem fit; And I reserve my own
liferent and I consent to registration for preservation: IN WITNESS
WHEREOF these presents written on this and the preceding page by
James Cameron, Clerk to Forsyth & Stewart, Solicitors, Elgin, are
subscribed by me at Elgin upon the Fifteenth day of February eighteen
hundred and eighty nine, before these witnesses, Hugh Stewart,
Solicitor in Elgin and Archibald Taylor, Clerk to the said Forsyth &
Stewart.*

This will caused considerable controversy among the heirs,
particularly in respect of the second purpose and is an excellent
illustration of a vesting problem. The will is archetypically Victorian in that it provides for the protection of the unmarried
daughters. The testatrix died in the 1890s but her last surviving
unmarried daughter, Isabella, survived until 1947. The second
purpose provides for the heritable property to be sold and divided
among the sons John, George and James. If these sons were to
predecease the "date of division" (the date of death of the last
unmarried daughter in 1947) their lawful issue could take their

share. All three sons predeceased the date. John and James both left lawful issue. The problem lay with George, who, as a young man, had gone abroad to seek his fortune. While living abroad, he married a German woman but died quite soon after the marriage. There were no children and it was believed that his widow had returned to Germany. The question was whether George's widow had any claim against the estate. Counsel's opinion was sought from Professor R. Candlish Henderson, Q.C., the leading expert on vesting and author of a much respected book on the subject.

His opinion was quite clear: the date of division was a certain day because, although the estate could not be divided until there ceased to an unmarried daughter, that day was bound to come eventually. All the unmarried daughters would eventually either marry or die unmarried. Because the bequest to the three sons was tied to a certain day, the legacy vested *a morte testatoris* but subject to defeasance in the case of any son who should (a) die before the date of division and (b) also leave issue. George did die before the date of division but he did not leave issue. Accordingly, his vested right was not subject to defeasance. The heirs of George's widow— unknown to the family and not a blood relative of the testator— could claim his one third share.

ACCRETION

Accretion (increasing by addition) is said to take place where one or more of several beneficiaries dies before the testator and his share is added on to the share of others, i.e. it "accresces".

The first place to look for guidance on this matter is the will itself and hopefully it will make the position clear. If it does not, the following fairly simple presumptions will apply. These presumptions derive from the case of *Paxton's Trs v Cowie* (1886) 13 R. 1191. It does not matter whether the property is heritable or moveable, nor is the nature of the bequest important, e.g. whether it is special, general or residuary, in liferent or in fee.

If the legacy is joint, e.g. ". . . to John and Jean", there will be accretion. Thus if John dies before the testator, the entire legacy goes to Jean, i.e. John's share accresces to Jean's.

If the legacy is several, e.g. ". . . to John and Jean equally between them" or ". . . to John and Jean share and share alike" (or similar words of severance), accretion does not apply. So if John dies before the testator, his share of the legacy would (probably) fall into the residue of the estate.

However, there is a pitfall for the unwary. If there is a legacy to a class of persons, e.g. "my nieces", even if there are words of severance, accretion would be presumed to apply. In *Robert's Trs v Roberts* (1903) 5 F. 541, a one-third share was left to each of three children. Dividing anything into three parts is a very clear example of severance. However, in context, accretion applied in respect of a predeceasing son's share, since it was a bequest to a class. A particular problem could arise where members of an apparent class are named individually; thus, ". . . to my sons John and James a one half share of . . . " may not be a class bequest, since they are named as individuals. Remember that all of these presumptions are subject to express provisions in the will.

A practical illustration may help, if we consider whether accretion would apply in the following circumstances, assuming that, in each case, party A dies before the testator.

(1) ". . . to A and B": this is a clear example of a joint legacy and A's share accresces to B.

(2) ". . . to A and B equally between them": because there are words of severance, accretion does not apply.

(3) ". . . to my nieces A and B": this is a joint legacy, so accretion would apply.

(4) ". . . to my nieces share and share alike": although there are words of severance, the bequest is to a class, so accretion would apply.

(5) ". . . to my nieces A and B equally between them": this is more problematic, since it is probably not a class gift, because the parties are individually named. Accretion would not apply, although the presumption would yield to the precise wording of the will.

Finally, accretion can take place as a result of events other than the death of a potential beneficiary. If, as happened in *Fraser's Trs v Fraser*, 1980 S.L.T. 211, a legacy is provided for A and B with words of severance, but the provision in favour of B is revoked by the testator, there is no accretion and the original provision in favour of B falls into intestate succession. If there are no words of severance, however, the bequest would be joint and A would take the entire share by accretion.

NUMBERING OF LEGACIES

Quite frequently, legacies in a will are numbered, normally just for administrative convenience. Unless the will makes it clear that the numbering indicates some form of priority (unlikely, but possible) no presumptions are raised. If there are insufficient resources in the estate to satisfy all the legacies in full, the rules on abatement (see Chapter 6) would apply.

CUMULATIVE AND SUBSTITUTIONAL LEGACIES

In cases where a will (or wills) provides two or more legacies to the same person, the question could arise as to whether these provisions are intended to be cumulative, i.e. all of them payable, or substitutional, one taking the place of the other. Obviously, the first place to look for guidance is the actual will itself. If there is no guidance, the following presumptions will apply:

If the legacies are contained in the same document and are for the same amount, it is presumed that the testator (and presumably his law agent!) did this in a moment of absent mindedness. In such a case the provisions are substitutional. In all other cases they are presumed to be cumulative. Illogical as it may be, it was held in *Gilles v Glasgow Royal Infirmary*, 1960 S.C. 438 that where there are two identical provisions of a share of residue, these were nevertheless cumulative. This seems to mean that a share of residue is not counted as a legacy.

It has already been shown that it is perfectly proper, and relatively common, for the same will to provide a specific legacy for a person and to give him a residuary provision as well.

Occasionally, a testator may leave two wills, both of which are valid. Provided both of these wills are valid, all provisions whether identical or not are cumulative, as shown in the case of *Arres' Trs v Mather* (1881) 9 R. 107. Fortunately, this problem does not often arise, as frequently the later will revokes the earlier expressly or by clear implication. However, a second will does not automatically revoke an earlier will as a matter of course. Problems arising where there is more than one will are explored in more detail in Chapter 9.

---

9. ALTERATIONS AND ADDITIONS

After someone has made a will, it is common and sensible practice for him to leave it with his law agent for safekeeping. It is certainly possible, even probable, that at some future date the testator may wish to make amendments to his will. Alternatively he may make entirely new provisions, particularly if circumstances change, e.g. if a main beneficiary were to die before the testator. Opportunities should be taken, at appropriate times, to update and review the settlement. Even today, many people are surprisingly resistant to making new wills, but this resistance may well disadvantage members of their family or, if they have no near family, their favourite charities. It is hard to believe that a 40-year-old will accurately reflects a testator's true wishes at the time of death.

Existing wills may be altered or superseded in a number of different ways, which will now be examined separately.

CODICIL

A codicil is a short deed granted by a testator making alterations to an original will. It is particularly useful where the original will is long and complicated. Perhaps in these days of word processing, it will technically be easier to retrieve a copy of an existing will on a computer file, make minor alterations and have the entire updated document signed of new. It remains to be seen how long solicitors will retain electronic records and how much use today's computer file will be in 20 years' time.

A codicil could be used, for example, to increase a general legacy to keep pace with inflation or to add a new grandchild to the list of beneficiaries. Sometimes a will may have several codicils. The tradition, in the days of writing or typewriting, was to engross the codicil on to the main will or, alternatively, to stitch it in as an appendix. It can just as easily be an entirely separate document, which is more likely in these days of word processing, but care should be taken to keep both documents together. If it is a true codicil, it will be quite clear that both the original will and the codicil(s) are to be read as one and that they are not two or more separate wills. In other words, the codicil should specifically refer to the original will and confirm the parts which are not expressly revoked.

A simple example of a codicil would be as follows:

I, JENNY BROWN, designed in the foregoing Will dated the Sixth day of February Nineteen Hundred and Ninety seven (hereinafter referred to as "my Will"), being desirous of making certain alterations and additions thereto, Do Hereby (First) increase the legacy to William Smith, designed in Clause Third of my Will to Ten Thousand pounds (£10,000); (Second) direct my executor to pay, as soon as convenient after my death but without interest to the date of payment, the sum of Five Thousand pounds (£5,000) to my housekeeper and companion, Mrs Euphemia Muckle, Eight Low Street, Aberfeldy. And except in so far as amended by this Codicil, I confirm my Will in all respects (*To be attested*)

REVOCATION OF PREVIOUS WILL

If a person makes a new will to replace an existing provision, it is important to revoke all prior wills, so that there is no doubt as to what the testator's true intentions actually were. It is difficult to know which result is worse—to have someone die and (against his wishes) to leave two wills which are both operative—or to leave a will and have the estate (or part of it) fall into intestate succession.

Revocation can be carried out in the following ways:

(1) The testator, if he wishes to revoke the entire will, may destroy the deed by completely tearing it up (or shredding it), either in person or by giving express authority to his law agent or some other person. This revokes the will, assuming that the testator possessed the *animus revocandi* (intention to revoke). If the destruction was accidental, or carried out during a period of the testator's insanity, it may not finally revoke the will.

If it can be shown that destruction of a will was unintentional or fraudulent it would be possible to have the missing will set up by raising an action to prove the tenor of the document in the Court of Session. It would generally be easier to prove that destruction had been carried out by someone other than the testator. Good evidence of the contents of a missing will would be a copy or a draft, but additional evidence of witnesses would also be required. However, written evidence is not absolutely essential since, if it were, proving the tenor of a will which had suffered fraudulent destruction would often be extremely difficult, even impossible.

It is important to notice one presumption applied by the courts. If it can be shown that a testator executed a will and that, thereafter, he retained that will in his own custody but at the time of his death it cannot be found, there is the presumption that he destroyed it *animo revocandi* (with the intention to revoke). Like most presumptions, it can be rebutted, but the burden of the proof is on the party who seeks to do so. In the old case of *Laing v Bruce* (1838) 1 D. 59, the deceased's will could not be found and it was presumed that it had been destroyed *animo revocandi*. The potential beneficiaries attempted to show that the testator had been insane for a period prior to her death. In fact, they were not able to do so and their action of proving the tenor failed. In *Clyde v Clyde*, 1958 S.C. 343, a testator made a will, favouring his nephew, and left the document with his solicitors. Some considerable time later—and several years before his eventual death—he requested his solicitor to send the will to him. At the time of his death, the will could not be found and it was held to have been intentionally destroyed by the testator.

A potential problem could arise where a second will is destroyed, or is proved to be invalid and an earlier valid will has also been destroyed. What is the status, if any, of the earlier will? In *Cullen's Exr v Elphinstone*, 1948 S.C. 662, such a problem arose. A second will was signed and, in accordance with professional practice, the earlier will was destroyed. It transpired that the second will was not properly executed and was thus invalid. The court held that although the earlier will had certainly been destroyed, it had not been validly revoked.

Occasionally, it is possible to encounter examples of what can only be described as partial destruction. What if there is a will, but parts of the text have been scored out or obliterated? It is obvious that this could easily have been done fraudulently, so there would need to be some evidence that the obliteration was carried out by the testator (or with the testator's express authority) and not by some unscrupulous third party.

Normally, the court would require some form of authentication of the deletion, such as initials, signature or written explanation. In each case, the court would also require to look at all the relevant facts and circumstances. In *Thomson's Trs v Bowhill Baptist Church*, 1956 S.L.T. 302, certain clauses in a will had been scored out, then physically cut out with scissors, the testator had signed near the gap and signed a written explanation above and below the gaps. In the circumstances, it was held that the missing clauses had been validly deleted.

(2) A common method of revocation is an express declaration in a later will that earlier wills are "hereby revoked". Generally speaking, a declaration of this kind is effective (although see the case of *Bruce's J.F. v Lord Advocate* below). If there is no express revocation—and the earlier will has not been destroyed in a regular manner—it may be that the two wills have to be read together. Of course, it is unlikely that this is what the testator would have wished, unless he perceived his second will as being in the nature of an extended codicil, in which case that fact ought to have been made clear.

In some cases, revocation (or partial revocation) may be implied in so far as the earlier will is inconsistent with the later one. A rule of thumb is that if the later will is a universal settlement, i.e. deals with the entire estate as one, without any other bequests, the earlier will is revoked by implication. However, if the two wills can be read together, the general rule is that they would both be effective. In *Duthie's Exrs v Taylor*, 1986 S.L.T. 142, a second will conveyed the testator's whole estate to trustees but made no direction as to the residue of the estate, although it did provide for certain legacies. The two wills were read together and most of the legacies in the earlier will were effective.

If it is claimed that a later will revokes an earlier will by implication, it appears that the party alleging such revocation requires to discharge a very heavy burden of proof. The general presumption seems, beyond doubt, to be that the two documents will be read as one unless there is an express revocation in the later will. In *Mitchell's Administratrix v Edinburgh Royal Infirmary*, 1928 S.C. 47, a codicil to a will was ambivalent (although professionally drafted) on the matter of revocation of certain provisions made in the principal will. The original provisions stood.

So, what happens if a testator signs a second will which expressly revokes previous wills, yet when he dies, the second will cannot be found but the first one can? Does this mean that the first will, having previously been expressly revoked, is revived and effective? This was the problem that faced the court in *Bruce's J.F. v Lord Advocate*, 1969 S.C. 296 (a multiplepoinding). In 1945, Mr Bruce signed a will, which remained with his law agents. In 1949, he signed a second will, revoking all previous wills but he retained the second will in his possession. At the time of his death, the second will could not be found. The presumption was raised that Bruce had destroyed the second will *animo revocandi*. So far, so good. But another problem arose in that the first will still existed. This first will had been revoked by the second will—but did destruction of the second will revive the first one? Not without some difficulty, the court decided that the first will was effective. Possibly the court was influenced by the fact that if someone bothers to make two wills over the course of his lifetime, he does not intend to die intestate. If the first will had been regularly destroyed *on the instructions of the testator*, this, coupled with the express revocation in the later will, would have ensured that it could not revive. A similar result would probably have arisen if the solicitor had been instructed to destroy the first will but had failed to do so, but the law is not beyond doubt on this matter.

(3) It has already been demonstrated in Chapter 8 that if a child successfully invokes the *conditio si testator*, his parent's will is entirely revoked. Generally speaking, any earlier wills which are expressly revoked by the will in question are not revived. The same result would seem to apply to any situation where the revocation of a specific will is the outcome of a court decree.

GOOD PROFESSIONAL PRACTICE

There is a clear moral emerging from what has just been examined. The best professional practice is, when a client signs a second will, to (1) ensure that there is a clause in the second will expressly revoking all previous testamentary writings; (2) ask the client for express instructions to destroy the earlier will; and (3) destroy it there and then in his presence.

MUTUAL WILLS

Mutual wills, in which two or more parties sign the same testamentary document, are rare in practice and certainly best avoided. The question that has exercised the courts on a few occasions is whether the document is contractual in nature or whether the parties are free to revoke their respective parts of the testamentary provisions. Such revocation might be before or after the death of the other party.

As a very general rule, a mutual will is no more than two or more wills run together. Thus the parties are free to revoke all or any of the testamentary provisions made by them individually. However, if the parties are spouses or civil partners, it is more likely that the terms of the document are contractual and unbreakable.

---

10. WILL SUBSTITUTES

SPECIAL DESTINATIONS

In Chapter 7, consideration was given to what is meant by a destination-over of a legacy. The special destination is rather different. At its simplest, a special destination is where property is held in common by two (or more) living parties in "joint names and survivor" (not merely joint names) or some similar arrangement. To understand this somewhat curious device, a little bit of history is required. Up until 1868, it was not possible to dispose of heritable property in Scotland by testamentary provision, unless certain rather technical steps were taken. The heritable property had to follow the feudal succession, which favoured the first-born and male. A will, accordingly, normally only dealt with moveable property (and, even until the passing of the 1964 Act, an executor could only confirm to moveable property).

Whatever criticisms people might wish to make of the legal profession, it could never be seriously suggested that lawyers lack inventiveness or initiative. As an owner of heritable property could not easily dispose of it by will, was there not some way round the problem? Necessity is the mother of invention. The legal profession came up with a solution, namely building a survivorship clause into the actual title to the property. So, if the property was held, for example, by "A and B and the survivor" or "A whom failing B", the general effect was testamentary. This was highly ingenious and, more importantly, it worked.

Since the need for such a device disappeared under the Titles to Land (Consolidation) Act 1868, section 20, which abolished restrictions on making testamentary provision over heritable property, one would have thought that the special destination would only have a limited remaining useful life. This has not been the result and, so far as may be seen, the special destination grew in popularity over the course of the 20th century. In some ways, its use has become a habit and there is divided opinion as to whether that habit is good or bad. Some solicitors recommend putting a special destination into the title of heritable property where parties are buying in more than one name almost as a matter of course. It is suggested that a special destination should only be included when there are clear and specific instructions from the client to do so.

It is important to make one distinction very clear. If a property is taken in the name of "A and B", this is not, nor does it imply, a special destination. If A dies, his half share of the property would have to be confirmed to in the usual way and be distributed either according to testate or intestate succession. Depending on the identity and relationship of the parties, B might not be A's heir. Any heritable property that passes under a special destination does not form part of the deceased's estate for the purposes of confirmation, although account is taken of it for the purposes of inheritance tax. Very occasionally, if a destination is unusually complicated, an executor may require to seek confirmation to the share for the limited purpose of conveying it to the beneficiary. In such a case, the value of the property is counted as nil and it is made clear that the executor is only confirming to it for this limited purpose. Otherwise, to confirm to heritable property passing under a special destination amounts to professional negligence.

A special destination was—and still is—particularly useful where the co-owners of heritable property are not spouses, whether they are cohabitees, friends or siblings, even taking into account recent legislation covering the succession of civil partners and cohabitees. Where there is a special destination, the succession to the property is clear. One could just as easily add that if people made proper wills, this would be an equally satisfactory solution and there would be no need to use a special destination. This, however, is probably the counsel of perfection.

There can be pitfalls in using the special destination. In *Christie's Exrx v Armstrong*, 1996 S.L.T. 948, Mr C and Ms A cohabited in a property in Rutherglen, which they had bought "in joint names and survivor". Mr C was actually married to another lady, much older than Ms A, and there were children of the marriage. Mr C and Ms A had granted a standard security over the property to a building society, from which they had borrowed the funds to finance the purchase. They had also assigned to the society, in further security, a life insurance policy on Mr C's life and this assignation had been duly intimated to the insurance company. The ink on this documentation was scarcely dry when Mr C died very unexpectedly. The insurance company paid the proceeds of the policy to the building society (which was the correct course). The proceeds were almost identical to the capital sum outstanding and there was a minor capital credit balance of around £30. The title to the house, of course, passed automatically to Ms A, under the special destination. Everyone might have lived happily ever after had not C's daughter, having been appointed as his executor-dative, raised her head above the parapet. She claimed her late father had, in effect, paid off the whole loan and that, as her father's executor, she was entitled to claim repayment of one half of that sum. The action was dismissed since the policy was not part of his estate at the time of his death (because it had been validly assigned to the lender), so he could not be considered as having paid the debt. If the policy had not been assigned in security, the result would have been different; clearly the deceased's estate would only, at the end of the day, have been liable for one half of the outstanding debt.

The question is bound to arise as to whether or not a special destination can be superseded by a later will. Suppose that title to property was taken in the name of "A and B and the survivor". Further suppose that A dies, but in his will he leaves his half-share of the property to C. This is a complex area but (at the risk of being over-simplistic) the general rule is that a later will does not wash out ("evacuate") an existing special destination. It certainly does not do so where the destination is contractual, i.e. where two co-owners have contributed to the cost, as is the case with many husband and wife destinations. The same would apply in the case of civil partners. If only one party has contributed to the purchase, that party does have power to evacuate the destination but the non-contributing party does not. If the funds were provided by a third party, neither party has the power to evacuate.

In any event, a post-1964 Act will cannot evacuate a special destination unless it contains (a) specific reference to the destination and (b) a declared intention to evacuate. It is also worth pointing out that at common law, a divorce did not automatically evacuate a special destination any more than it revoked a will. In *Gardner's Exrs v Raeburn*, 1996 S.L.T. 745, a couple divorced; the title to their house was in joint names and survivor. As part of the divorce settlement, the wife conveyed her half share to the husband (in fact, he paid her for the half-share). Unfortunately, the half-share belonging to the husband remained subject to the special destination. When he died, this half share passed to his former wife. This result almost certainly did not reflect the true wishes of the husband. To prevent such a situation arising, it became good practice to ensure that *both* parties conveyed the entire property to the party who was taking the title. This ensured that the destination was properly washed out of the title.

Section 19 of the 2006 Act changes the common law position by providing that, where there is a title in the name of person A and person B (A's spouse) and the survivor, or to A, B, another party and their survivor or survivors, or to A with a provision that the property is to pass to B on A's death, then, in the event of divorce or annulment (but not separation), B shall be counted as not having survived A (for the purposes of the destination only). A purchaser in good faith and for value is protected in the event that he buys the property from B, when, of course, B has no title due to the divorce of the parties. The Act does permit parties to opt out of the statutory provisions by express provision in the destination that it will not be evacuated by subsequent divorce or annulment.

An interesting problem arose in the case of *Redfern's Exrs v Redfern*, 1996 S.L.T. 900, where spouses signed a separation agreement renouncing any rights of succession in the estate of the other and agreeing to sell their house and share the proceeds. Before the house could be sold, Mr R died. The property was subject to a survivorship destination. The question at issue was obvious: did the entire heritable property now belong to Mrs R or had the destination been evacuated by the separation agreement? It was held that rights of succession (at least in this context) included those normally passing under a special destination. The separation agreement had effectively evacuated the destination.

However, although the general effect of a special destination is testamentary, it is not actually a will and, as shown above, is not (generally) superseded by a later testamentary writing. The fact that it is not strictly testamentary was the cause of what may seem an odd result in the case of *Barclays Bank Ltd v McGreish*, 1983 S.L.T. 344. Mr and Mrs M held the title to their heritable property in joint names and survivor. Mrs M had provided all of the original funds for the purchase. The bank obtained a decree against Mr M's half share but, before they could enforce it, Mr M died. It was held that the special destination not only transferred his half share of the house to his wife but also did so free of debt. The reasoning behind this "have your cake and eat it" result was that as the property did not pass through the hands of the executor, it could not be subjected to debts constituted against the estate. The soundness of this reasoning has, however, been doubted and was not followed in the sheriff court case of *Fleming's Trs v Fleming*, 2000 S.L.T. 406.

It is also possible to have incorporeal moveable property subject to a special destination. Examples include shares in a company or bonds. The mere fact that incorporeal moveable property is held in more than one name does not imply a special destination, at least in Scotland.

With heritable property, the special destination actually moves the ownership of the property to whoever is "called", i.e. the survivor, and no conveyance is required unless the destination is unusually complicated. To be made into a real right, a heritable title normally must either be recorded in the General Register of Sasines or (more commonly now) registered in the Land Register. It is well established that, in the case of a straightforward survivorship destination, the share belonging to the deceased passes automatically at the time of his death (*Bisset v Walker*, 26 Nov. 1799, Fac. Coll.). In the case of an existing sasine title, no further formality is required and, perhaps surprisingly, the public record will continue to show all original proprietors as owners unless and until such time as the survivor disposes of his share. In the case of a registered title, it is possible (and highly desirable) to request the Keeper of the Registers to rectify the Land Register to show the effect of the operation of the destination.

In the case of incorporeal moveable property passing under a special destination, the situation is rather more blurred and, in practice, a share of the property is often confirmed to as though it was not subject to a special destination. In the case of a deposit receipt (and probably in the case of a bank account) the survivor has more of an administrative role and is only entitled to uplift the subjects. He must then account for the proceeds to the deceased's executor. In *Dinwoodie's Exrx v Carruther's Exr* (1895) 23 R. 234, parties A and B had a deposit receipt for £450 in name of "A and B and survivor". In fact, A had contributed £50 and B the remaining £400. It was held that A was entitled to uplift the funds on B's death, but A only owned what he had put in, plus relative interest as the balance of the funds belonged to B's executor. In practice, special destinations are far less common in the case of moveable property.

Finally, it is important to notice that a special destination only operates where one party actually survives the other. Thus if husband and wife hold property in joint names and survivor and both are killed in a common calamity, neither is presumed to survive the other, unless evidence shows otherwise. Thus the special destination could not operate and their executors would require to confirm to the respective half-shares.

NOMINATIONS

The deceased may have nominated another party to receive certain funds, such as a bank account or benefits under a pension scheme, on the event of his death. Such a nomination, like a special destination, has a general testamentary effect but it is not necessary for the executor to confirm to such funds. A true nomination will be based on a statutory provision, which will require to be checked out in each particular case. In some cases (not many) the funds may still require to be first delivered to the executor.

In fact, payments of relatively modest sums to a deceased's next-of-kin are frequently allowed by financial institutions as a matter of privilege, rather than right. If a holder of funds belonging to a deceased person chooses to pay them to anyone other than an executor with confirmation, he generally does so at his own risk and a confirmed executor would have the right to demand payment again. Usually the maximum value to be paid out under a nomination will be £5,000. The payer will require evidence of death and entitlement. The beneficiary may be required to sign an indemnity, in case an executor with confirmation appears at a later date.

Generally speaking, a nomination is not evacuated by a subsequent will, although the nomination itself may be revoked by the appropriate statutory documentation. Unlike a will, the nomination is invalidated if the nominator subsequently marries or remarries. Similarly to a testamentary provision, if the beneficiary (nominee) dies before the nominator, the nomination simply falls.

POLICIES OF INSURANCE

If—and only if—a policy of life insurance is written under the Married Women's Policies of Assurance (Scotland) Act 1880 (as amended), it counts as a separate estate and is not confirmed to nor does it need to be accounted for, for the purposes of inheritance tax. The 1880 Act, as amended, applies to both husbands and wives. The spouse who takes out such a policy is counted as a trustee and the beneficiaries have vested rights from the time the policy is taken out. The policy proceeds are payable to the surviving spouse and/or children on production of the death certificate. It is not necessary for the policy to make specific mention of the 1880 Act, provided the creation of the trust is clear.

ANTE-NUPTIAL MARRIAGE CONTRACT TRUSTS

These somewhat cumbersome arrangements were popular with our Victorian forefathers, particularly among the more prosperous classes. It has to be remembered that, in former times, married women were often treated as little better than wayward children when it came to the administration of their own property. A lady of means might have had much to lose if her fortune was entirely at the mercy of her husband.

Shortly before the marriage, the woman transferred her property to trustees but, normally, retained an alimentary liferent in her own favour. (The right of a woman to do this was abolished under the Law Reform (Husband and Wife) (Scotland) Act 1984.) Since the consideration of the contract was the marriage taking place, that contract could not come into operation until such time as the marriage was actually solemnised. However, once the contract came into force, it was irrevocable, on the grounds that it gave rights to children *nascituri* (yet to be born), unless the contract itself gave express powers of revocation. Some marriage contracts contain provisions that are clearly intended to be testamentary. It appears to be the case (*Barclay's Trs v Watson* (1903) 5 F. 926) that such provisions are always revocable, even if the contract declares them to be irrevocable.

DONATIONS *MORTIS CAUSA*

Donations (gifts) given in contemplation of death are, in themselves, not uncommon, especially when small items of sentimental value are involved. An elderly person may wish to pass such items to members of family or close friends and this is scarcely controversial. Leaving aside the question of liability to inheritance tax, the question may arise as to whether it counts as an out-and-out gift or a donation *mortis causa*. If it is an out-and-out gift, it is generally irrevocable. If it is a donation *mortis causa*, the donor can revoke the donation during his own lifetime. If the recipient predeceases, the donation reverts to the donor. In the case of an insolvent estate, the value of the donation could be reclaimed by the executor or trustee. A donation *mortis causa* ranks after legal rights, but before legacies.

Thus, a donation *mortis causa* is somewhere between a straightforward gift and a legacy. The law always presumes against donation and there may be difficulties of proof. Although the law requires writing to convey particular property (such as an interest in land), writing is not required as a matter of proof of donation. Most donations are not, in practice, fortified by written documentation. The normal rule in donation *mortis causa* is that there has to be delivery (or equivalent) to the recipient, although the rule has not always been as strictly applied as it would in the case of donation *inter vivos*.

---

11. INTERPRETATION OF WILLS

This is a complex area in its own right and only the generalities can be covered in a book of this size. The reader will already have deduced that when anyone has the duty of interpreting the wishes of a testator, the obvious and logical first step is to read the will extremely carefully to see *exactly* what it says.

THE GENERAL RULE

As a very general rule, if a court is called upon to interpret a will, it does so intrinsically, i.e. within the four corners of the document. The question, in other words, is "What does the will actually say?" This may well be different from what beneficiaries or potential beneficiaries might wish it to say.

EXTRINSIC EVIDENCE

Extrinsic evidence, i.e. evidence from outside the four corners of the deed, will not, as a general rule, be permitted when it comes to ascertaining the testator's intention. To put this another way, the court will not entertain evidence being brought as to what the testator thought he meant by certain words where these words, in themselves, are perfectly clear. It is obvious that if such evidence were competent, the system could be open to abuse by disappointed prospective beneficiaries trying to stake a claim. A testator is presumed to use words in their normal manner, unless the context shows otherwise, as it did in *Yule's Trs,* 1981 S.L.T. 250, where "child" was interpreted as meaning a grandchild in that particular context.

Having said all that, there are times when the court will allow extrinsic evidence. This would be allowed if it was claimed that the will had been signed under facility and circumvention or undue influence—or even that the will was a forgery or had not been properly executed. If extrinsic evidence could not be brought forward in such cases, there would be no possible means of challenge.

There may also (and this is where it becomes rather more technical) be cases where extrinsic evidence may be allowed to clarify what was *known* to the testator at the time he signed the will. This is a very different matter from attempting to show that the testator actually meant something different from what he expressly said. If the wording of the will makes perfect sense on its own, without going outside its four corners, that wording will stand. Thus, in *Fortunato's J.F. v Fortunato*, 1981 S.L.T. 277, a clear bequest of a public house did not include other property belonging to the testator within the same building.

If the will is written in a foreign language or in some form of code, external evidence by way of translation is permitted, which is no more than common sense.

Among the range of factors that would need to be clear to a testator are whom he intended to benefit and which property he had in mind. In such cases, minor errors in description need not be fatal and the true facts could allow for extrinsic evidence being introduced. In *Wedderspoon v Thomson's Trs* (1824) 3 S. 396, Thomson had left £500 to "Janet Keiller or Williamson, confectioner in Dundee". There was no such person. The legacy was successfully claimed by Agnes Keiller or Wedderspoon, who was married to a confectioner in Dundee, the court being satisfied, by extrinsic evidence, that only a clerical error was involved. In the related case of *Keiller v Thomson's Trs.* (1826) 4 S. 724, the same Thomson had left a legacy to "William Keiller, confectioner in Dundee". Again, there was no such person. There were, however, two possible claimants, William Keiller, confectioner in Montrose and James Keiller, confectioner in Dundee. The court considered extrinsic evidence and decided that the testator had intended the legacy to go to James Keiller of Dundee.

In *Cathcart's Trs v Bruce*, 1923 S.L.T. 722, a legacy was to "General Alexander Fairlie Bruce". There were two possible beneficiaries, General Alexander J. Bruce and Mr Alexander F. Bruce. Extrinsic evidence allowed the legacy to be paid to the General.

Similar rules will apply if the subject matter of the legacy is in doubt, e.g. if a testator owns two houses in Glebe Street, Anyburgh and he bequeaths "my house in Glebe Street, Anyburgh"—which one is intended? If it is not clear from the will, the court will allow extrinsic evidence. If the identity of the legatee or the subject matter is still in doubt after leading extrinsic evidence, the legacy will be of no effect.

In cases of doubt, the court will, if possible, interpret the provision in a way that avoids total or partial intestacy. In *Magistrates of Dundee v Morris* (1858) 3 Macq. 134, testamentary trustees were directed to set up a school (which eventually became Morgan Academy) but no actual cash sum was stated. However, as the will did specify the size of the proposed school, the amount of the legacy required could be ascertained and the provision did not fail from uncertainty.

DISPOSITIVE DISCRETION

It is not unusual for a testator to give his executors or testamentary trustees some degree of dispositive discretion, meaning that they have discretion, within certain parameters, as to who might benefit and/or by how much. Thus a testator might provide a sum of money to be divided among "such charitable organisations favouring orphaned children as my trustees, in their absolute discretion, may select". In such a case, the general intention of the testator is perfectly clear since a class of beneficiaries is identified. However, a testator cannot entirely delegate his power to test. If the discretion is completely open-ended, the bequest may fail from uncertainty. In *Anderson v Smoke* (1898) 25 R. 493, there was a direction to trustees to dispose of the residue of the estate in any way they should think fit, but this provision was void from uncertainty. Dispositive discretion cannot be exercised by an executor-dative, even if appointed to a testate estate. In *Angus' Exrx v Batchan's Trs,* 1949 S.C. 335, a lady left a home-made will which provided for the residue of the estate to be given to "charities". The will failed to appoint an executor. It was held that an executor-dative does not have dispositive discretion and the bequest to charities failed from uncertainty. Had the will appointed an executor, the direction would almost certainly have been valid. Similar rules would apply where the court has appointed a judicial factor. In *Robbie's J.F. v Macrae* (1893) 20 R. 358, the deceased had directed her executors to pay the residue of her estate to such charities as they thought proper within a stated class of charities. On the face of it, this direction was both valid and sensible. Unfortunately, all of her executors died before exercising the discretion and a judicial factor was appointed by the court. It was held that the discretion could not be exercised by a judicial factor.

There is a considerable body of case law on the legal viability of such phrases as "public, religious, educational and charitable purposes" which is beyond the realistic scope of this book.

PRECATORY BEQUESTS

Occasionally, a problem can arise when the testator does not indicate clearly whether he is merely expressing a wish or giving an actual instruction. Such an expression of wish is known as a precatory bequest, from the Latin *precari* (to pray). The problem might arise most frequently in a home-made will, where a testator is more likely to use words such as "would like" or "prefer" rather than more assertive verbs such as "instruct" or "direct" found in professionally drafted wills. The obvious question is whether or not such a precatory provision is binding in law, apart from any possible moral obligation. The rough rule of thumb seems to be that if a wish is expressed to an executor or testamentary trustee, it is more likely to be taken as an instruction than if it is expressed to a beneficiary. Thus in *Barclay's Exr v McLeod* (1880) 7 R. 477, a desire expressed to an inheriting spouse that she should make testamentary provisions for other relatives was not legally binding. On the other hand in *Reid's Trs v Dawson*, 1915 S.C. (HL) 47, where a testator "preferred" his trustees to pay a capital sum to a beneficiary, this was held to be an instruction and thus a valid bequest. There may also be cases where a request or instruction to an executor cannot be carried out. In *Milne v Smith*, 1982 S.L.T. 129, the testator provided a legacy to his son in the hope that the partnership, of which the father had been part, would be continued by the son. This was beyond the powers of the executor to fulfil and the legacy was paid without being subject to conditions.

IDENTIFYING A BENEFICIARY

The beneficiary, or "object", of a legacy is usually identifiable without difficulty and, as shown above, minor errors in names or designations are not normally fatal. Potential problems can arise in legacies to relations. In *Robertson's J.F. v Robertson*, 1968 S.L.T. 32, a legacy to "dependants" failed due to the uncertainty of that word. In most cases, a legacy to "next-of-kin" means to those who would have been entitled under intestacy, unless the will bears otherwise, but would not include representatives. However, a bequest to "heirs" would include next-of-kin and representatives.

At common law, a "child" meant only legitimate offspring unless the context clearly indicated otherwise. As a result of the 1964 Act, adopted children are included, as are illegitimate children under the Law Reform (Miscellaneous Provisions) (Scotland) Act 1968 and the Law Reform (Parent and Child) (Scotland) Act 1986. The status of illegitimacy was finally removed by the 2006 Act. Wills executed before these respective statutory provisions came into force are not subject to these presumptions.

"Issue" includes children as well as direct descendants, such as grandchildren or great grandchildren, who can represent a predeceasing parent or ancestor or claim their vested right.

Until the Age of Minority (Scotland) Act 1969, "full age" was the traditional 21 years, but was dropped to 18 by the Act. Interpretation depends on whether the will was signed before or after the Act came into force. The minimum age for making a will is 12. A young person aged 16 or 17 can grant a valid discharge, deed of variation or a renunciation of legal rights; but has until age 21 to challenge it as a prejudicial transaction. In practice, a straightforward receipt for legitim or for a legacy, paid in full, would not give rise to any such claim. The minimum age for an executor is 16.

Apart from the statutory provisions in the preceding paragraphs, the general presumption is that no matter how old a will is, it indicates the wishes of the deceased at the time of death. This presumption is not always helpful or even strictly accurate. Particular problems can arise with spouses. A spouse may predecease or the parties may divorce. In itself, divorce does not revoke a will (although it does now revoke a special destination). If there is a legacy to "my wife Jean", but the parties have divorced since the will was signed, does Jean still inherit? If, as in *Couper's J.F. v Valentine*, 1976 S.L.T. 83, the designation "wife" only counts as a personal identification, she would still inherit. If the will contains a suspensive condition such as "to my wife Jean, provided we are still married at the time of my death", clearly she could not inherit. Probably, a bequest to "my wife", without any name being applied, would count as a family rather than a personal provision and would favour the person to whom the testator was married at the time of his death.

A related, but separate, question is which law applies to a will— that which applied at the time of signature or at the time of death? Again, subject to the statutory presumptions noted above in connection with legitimacy, adoption and age of majority, the general rule is that the applicable law is that which applies at the date of the testator's death. This means that if the law changes in the period between the death of the testator and a subsequent vesting, the law would still be as at the date of the testator's death (*Wright's Trs v Callender*, 1993 S.L.T. 556).

12. THE EXECUTOR'S ROLE AND DUTIES

WHAT TO DO AFTER A DEATH TAKES PLACE

When a person dies at home or in hospital, a doctor will normally issue a medical certificate confirming the place, cause and time of the death. Alternatively, he may be required to report the death to the procurator fiscal where it is sudden, suspicious, accidental, unexpected or unexplained—or in cases that give rise to serious public concern. The procurator fiscal makes such enquiry as he sees fit and, in the majority of cases, allows a death certificate to be issued so that normal funeral arrangements can proceed. In some cases, he may request a post mortem examination, in which case he need not ask the permission of the next-of-kin. In appropriate situations, he may arrange for a fatal accident enquiry.

The death must be registered by the Registrar of Births, Marriages and Deaths within eight days. This includes all deaths that take place in Scotland, whatever the nationality of the deceased. The death can be registered with the local registrar for the district within which the person died or with the local registrar for the district where he normally lived, whichever is more convenient. The death may be registered by the deceased's spouse or civil partner, a relative through marriage or civil partnership, anyone present when the person died, the executor or the occupier of premises within which the death took place. If no one is available from this list, the death may be registered by anyone possessing the information required.

The most important document the registrar requires is the death certificate. He will also require information about the deceased's parentage and marriage status. Ideally, this information can be provided by the production of birth, marriage or civil partnership certificates, although this is not always possible at short notice. In addition, he will require information about the deceased's pension or other income from public funds. He will also ask who the deceased's medical practitioner was. Once registration of the death is complete, the registrar will issue a certificate (Form 14) to pass to the funeral director and another certificate (Form 334/S1) to pass to social security agencies. Registering a death is free, but if an extract of the death certificate is required (which it normally is) a charge is made. It should be remembered that it is an offence to pass off a copy of an official extract as though it were an original. Whilst official agencies, banks and insurance companies often legitimately photocopy the extract for their own records, they will invariably request sight of the official extract.

In the event of someone dying abroad, the death will be registered in accordance with the requirements of that country. However, it is good practice also to register the death with the British Consul so that the public record of death will eventually find its way back to Scotland.

One potentially difficult and sensitive area that can arise is the question of donation of organs from a deceased person. At common law, the wishes of a deceased person as to the disposal of all or part of his remains, even when contained in a will, can be over-ruled by the next-of-kin. It is not uncommon for someone to make a provision, usually in his will, for his remains to be used for medical research. This wish need not strictly be followed by his next-of-kin although, in practice, such provisions have usually been discussed previously with members of the family. Normally, the remains are given a funeral within three years of death.

Time will be of the essence in removal of any organs for transplant and the practice in hospitals for some time has been for a dedicated and trained official, called a transplant co-ordinator, to approach members of the family in a sensitive manner.

At the time of writing, the Human Tissue (Scotland) Act 2006 has recently come into force. As with all new legislation, it will take some time to bed down and to be interpreted by the courts. The general effect of the legislation is that a person may now provide that body parts can be removed for transplantation or research, even if his next-of-kin would prefer otherwise. In practice this will normally only arise when a person dies in hospital. The basic purpose of the new law is to ensure that the person's wishes about donation are respected. A person can express his wishes in various ways, such as use of a donor card, an entry on the National Health Service Organ Donor Register, an express provision in his will, or other written or verbal instructions. These wishes or instructions are given the generic title "authorisations" under the new law. If there is such an authorisation, the hospital staff may proceed to harvest the organs, but only after due enquiry into the donor's medical or social history in case there is anything that might make his organs unsuitable for transplantation.

Where the deceased has not left any authorisation, the transplant co-ordinator will approach the nearest relative (as defined in the Act) to enquire whether or not he will authorise removal of body parts for transplantation. The relative may give or withhold authorisation, based on what he knows of his deceased relative's views on the matter.

Increasingly, cremation is being used as a means of disposing of the dead. This involves more written preliminaries than is the case with interment. An application form has to be completed, accompanied by two certificates signed by doctors, plus a certificate signed by the medical referee for the crematorium. If someone dies abroad, the Scottish Executive Health Department has to grant an order before the remains can be cremated in Scotland.

THE APPOINTMENT OF THE EXECUTOR

Executors come in two main categories. If the deceased died testate, the will should have nominated an executor. Provided the named individual is willing and legally competent to act, he will assume the title of executor-nominate. There are occasions where a nominated executor declines to act, becomes *incapax* (incapable of carrying out the duties) or dies before taking up office. The Executors (Scotland) Act 1900, section 3, provides that, in any of these eventualities, the deemed executors-nominate are the testamentary trustees. However, frequently there are no such trustees, or if there are, they are the same persons as the executors. In such a case the office of executor, under the same statutory provision, falls on any general disponee, universal legatee or residuary legatee. In context, a general legatee is found where the estate is a mixture of heritage and moveables. In the case of a universal legatee, the estate is entirely moveable. A residuary legatee is explained in Chapter 7. If there are several legatees, they are all required to accept or decline the office expressly. If the will makes no provision for an executor, the procedure for appointment is the same as under intestate succession.

If the deceased died intestate, it will be necessary to petition the sheriff to appoint an executor, usually from among the next-of-kin, as set out in Chapter 4. In this case, the executor is called an executor-dative.

It goes without saying that a will is an important document. It makes sense to register it either in the Books of Council and Session (sometimes referred to as the Register of Deeds) in Edinburgh or in the books of the local sheriff court. The latter is slightly cheaper but the outcome is exactly the same in both cases. The original will is retained in perpetuity and becomes part of the public records of Scotland. A certified photocopied extract is issued which has the same legal status as the original, no more and no less. Thus if the will is open to challenge, it remains so. Registration does not make it any more "legal".

THE EFFECT OF CONFIRMATION

An executor cannot proceed to intromit with the estate until he has obtained confirmation from the sheriff. This is often misunderstood by the lay person. Thus, even although pressurised by members of the family to start distribution immediately after the funeral is over (if not sooner), the executor must firmly decline to do so. The confirmation is, in fact, the executor's legal title to intromit. The process starts with the executor completing a detailed inventory of the estate belonging to the deceased on the appropriate form. There is now only one form in use: Form C1. This inventory has a two-fold purpose of calculating whether any inheritance tax ("IHT") will be payable and of obtaining actual confirmation. If it appears that IHT will be payable, a Form IHT200 must also be completed. Both forms will then be sent to the Capital Taxes Office. When the provisional amount of IHT has been paid, the Office returns the Form C1, duly receipted and bearing a reference number, to the executors so that confirmation can proceed.

As outlined in Chapter 1, there is no IHT due on transfers between spouses or civil partners during their lifetimes or after death. Other transfers of property made more than seven years before death are similarly exempt. Debts and funeral expenses can also be deducted from the total value of the estate in calculating IHT. At the time of writing the IHT threshold is £285,000 (2006/2007 tax year), but this figure normally changes every year. Other exemptions and rules can also change. It is anticipated that the threshold will rise to £300,000 in 2007/2008, £312,000 in 2008/2009, £325,000 in 2009/2010 and £350,000 in 2010/2011. IHT is payable at the rate of 40 per cent of any excess in the net estate over the current threshold. Executors may well have to obtain a bridging loan to pay the tax.

When the sheriff issues confirmation, this is, to all intents and purposes, a copy of the inventory previously lodged by the executor but with an official warrant to the executor to intromit with the estate. If an executor (or anyone else) intromits with the property of the deceased without having confirmation, this intromission is counted as being vitious, which means that the vitious intromitter has to take personal liability for the debts of the deceased.

In carrying out his duties, an executor acts as the representative of the deceased. He is debtor to the deceased's creditors and creditor to the deceased's debtors and is entitled to sue for the recovery of debts due to the deceased. He may have to perform or conclude contracts undertaken by the deceased, although not if they involve an element of *delectus personae* (choice of person), i.e. where the personal skill or qualities of the deceased were relied on. An obvious example is the deceased's contract of employment, which dies with him.

A trust disposition and settlement may appoint the same person(s) as executor(s) and as trustee(s). This is perfectly in order and, indeed, quite normal. Although the two functions do overlap, they are distinct in law. If the testator appoints only trustees, such trustees are also entitled to seek confirmation as executors under the Executors (Scotland) Act 1900.

Once the inventory has been prepared (and any IHT paid) the executor can proceed to apply for confirmation. This is achieved by lodging the signed inventory with the sheriff clerk of the commissariot in which the deceased was domiciled, accompanied by the will appointing the executor-nominate or, in the case of an executor-dative, a bond of caution. Such a bond, issued by an insurance company, is a guarantee that the executor-dative will make the estate furthcoming, as explained in Chapter 4. If the executor-dative is the surviving spouse or civil partner whose prior rights will exhaust the entire estate, such a bond is not required. It is not necessary to lodge an extract of the decree appointing the executor-dative. In practice, such decrees are rarely extracted. The sheriff clerk will, in due course, issue the confirmation.

Armed with this document, the executor now has title to collect and ingather all the listed property, both heritable and moveable, which belonged to the deceased (apart from heritable property passing under a survivorship destination). The confirmation (or separate certificate of confirmation for any individual item on the inventory) can now be exhibited to whoever is in possession or custody, or whoever registers the item, such as a bank. The item will be encashed, sold, endorsed into the executor's name or transferred to a beneficiary. As money comes into the hands of the executor, he may proceed to pay off debts due by the deceased.

English companies will not note on a share certificate the trust capacity of any trustees. This is not because companies registered in England are disobliging, but is due to the application of the Companies Act 1985 section 360. This statutory provision does not apply in Scotland, where the fact that shares are held in trust may be entered on the register of members (shareholders). However, the fact that a trust's existence is disclosed in this way does not confine the liability of the trustees to the amount of the trust estate under their care (see Chapter 13). Thus the different practices in Scotland and England make little real difference. Normally, of course, the only liability of members of a limited company is to pay any calls due on shares.

It is not uncommon for an executor to find that he has omitted or even just undervalued or misdescribed part of the estate under his charge, e.g. a bank passbook may be found which the deceased had hidden away and of which the executor had no knowledge. In such a case, if confirmation has already been granted, the executor will prepare a corrective inventory incorporating the additional item for submission to the Capital Taxes Office and then the sheriff clerk. The executor will be granted an "eik" (pronounced "eek") to his confirmation. An eik is simply an additional confirmation that supplements or corrects the original document. If the original executor has died and additional property is discovered, it is not competent for his successor to apply for an eik. Instead, the new executor would be able to apply for confirmation *ad omissa* (in respect of things omitted).

If all the executors in whose favour the confirmation was granted die or become incapacitated, creditors and other interested parties can apply for confirmation *ad non executa* (in respect of property not administered) and this authorises them to complete the administration of the estate.

If the deceased owned estate outwith Scotland, confirmation may not be acceptable in that country. Thus it may be necessary for the confirmation to be re-sealed in the probate register of that country. A Scottish confirmation is recognised throughout the United Kingdom by virtue of reciprocal arrangements (Administration of Estates Act 1971) and may include property in England, Wales or Northern Ireland, if the deceased had his domicile in Scotland.

DRAFTING THE INVENTORY

Drafting the inventory is a practical skill that cannot be obtained merely by reading books. Nevertheless, it is useful to make a few comments about this crucial part of the executry process. It stands to reason that every estate is different. The following are only very general rules which, according to best legal practice, should only be applied after due care and enquiry.

An executor does not want to overvalue the estate—the greater the value, the higher the confirmation dues. Even more important is the need to mitigate the possible demands of IHT. It is, however, equally important to ensure that the valuations on the inventory are realistic and honest. It is not only a waste of time, but it is also professional malpractice for a solicitor knowingly to enter an item at less than its true value. Having said that, valuation is not always an exact science. The general rule is that all assets are valued at open market value as at the date of death.

When listing the estate on the inventory form, the order to be followed is:

Estate in Scotland (heritable first)
Estate in England and Wales
Estate in Northern Ireland
Summary for confirmation
Estate elsewhere

Each item should be consecutively numbered. At the end of the list of property in the United Kingdom, the summary referred to above appears. An example might be:

SUMMARY FOR CONFIRMATION

Heritable Estate in Scotland	£96,000.00
Moveable Estate in Scotland	£21,798.68
Personal Estate in England and Wales	£23,291.02
	£141,089.70

Heritable Property
How heritable property is described for confirmation is partly a matter of taste when it comes to an existing sasine title. The description must be sufficient to identify the subjects, so that "Flat, 10 Glebe Street, Anyburgh" would be adequate. However, it is not altogether satisfactory if, say, it is a flat in a tenement house where several properties might share the same street number. It would normally be better to use at least a general conveyancing description, e.g. "ALL and WHOLE the westmost first floor flat forming part of the tenement dwellinghouse entering by the common passage and stair at Ten Glebe Street, Anyburgh in the County of Naeplace together with all rights and privileges effeiring thereto".

The above assumes a sasine title. If the title has previously been registered, a general description is not needed but it is essential that the registered title number is quoted, e.g. "Flat, 10 Glebe Street, Anyburgh registered as title number NAE998765". In the case of an existing sasine title, conveying the property to a beneficiary does not induce a first registration and any disposition in his favour will continue to be recorded in the appropriate Division of the General Register of Sasines. If the property is to be sold by the executors, the disposition to the buyer will induce a first registration.

It has become almost invariable practice for married couples, cohabitees or others who share the use of heritable property to take title in joint names. The difference between holding in joint names and holding in joint names and survivor has already been covered in Chapter 10. At the risk of repetition, in the former case a one half *pro indiviso* share ought to be confirmed to when the

first of the parties dies. In the latter case, the half-share passes
automatically under the special destination and is not confirmed to.
The value of the property has to be accounted for elsewhere in the
inventory Form C1, but only for the purposes of calculating any
IHT that may be due.

Because a mortgage is a heritable debt, it is deducted from the
heritable estate at this stage. Thus, if a property was valued at
£96,000 but there was an outstanding secured loan of £50,000, this
would be shown in the inventory and the net value would be the
figure for confirmation purposes, along the following lines:

ALL and WHOLE the dwellinghouse, *etc.*   £96,000
less outstanding secured loan due to, *etc.*   £50,000
                                             ─────────
                                                      £46,000

Occasionally, a deceased may have been a creditor in a standard
security, although most heritable creditors are financial institutions.
As demonstrated in Chapter 1, the value of the standard security
counts as a moveable asset for the purposes of confirmation but it
counts as a heritable asset in respect of legal rights or taxation. The
obvious effect is that legal rights cannot be claimed out of the value
of the security, as they can only be claimed out of the net moveable
assets.

Cash in house
Any balance of cash in the deceased's possession, no matter how
small, should be handed over to the executor and accounted for in
the inventory.

Household furniture and personal effects
It is a matter of judgement whether it is necessary to go to the
expense of a professional valuation. If IHT is likely to be payable, a
valuation on a professional basis may be required, otherwise a
reasonable approximation will probably be adequate. It is not
usually necessary to list all the separate items of furnishing within
the deceased's house; one global sum is sufficient. If the furnishings
have been professionally valued, the valuer will normally produce a
detailed inventory of items. Reference may be made to this report
on the Form C1—something along the following lines:

Furnishings in house, as valued by Messrs Black &
Whyte   £2,3010.00

The valuation is what the effects are worth as at date of death, not
what it might cost to replace them of new (as in an insurance
policy). In the case of one of a married couple or civil partnership

dying, the furniture and effects in the house would be confirmed to in respect of a half-share, unless the true facts were different. Items such as jewellery, antiques or specialist hobby equipment may require professional valuation.

Motor car
As explained in Chapter 4, in professional practice a motor car is not normally counted as part of the household effects. A car may be valued by using one of the trade guides or obtaining a professional valuation. The car should be identified by its make, model and registration number. There are no presumptions about half-shares in cars.

Bank and building society Accounts
These figures can be obtained from the institution itself with interest accrued to date of death. Having been informed of the death of its customer, the institution should freeze the account, unless it is a joint account. Irrespective of the location of the head office, if the deceased used a local branch, count the monies as property in Scotland. If an account is held in joint names, as is common with spouses, and one of the holders dies, the inventory should state the proportion contributed by the deceased. There is no presumption about half-shares.

National Savings
These are entered as property in Scotland, irrespective of their centre of administration. National Savings Certificates are valued free of charge by the appropriate National Savings Centre and this applies to other National Savings products. Premium Savings Bonds are valued at par, although they remain eligible for a prize draw for a period of 12 months after date of death and should not be liquidated before that date.

Company shares
All companies in the United Kingdom count as British but the location of a company's registered office determines whether shares are counted as property in Scotland or England and Wales.

Valuation of shares in a publicly quoted plc is straightforward and, in practice, is usually carried out by a stockbroker. The stockbroker should be informed that the valuation is for the purpose of confirmation. The shares are valued as at date of death. The lower of the two valuation figures quoted in the *Financial Times* is taken and that figure is "quartered up". An example would be if shares were quoted at 380p/384p. The basis of the valuation would be 380p plus one quarter of the difference between the higher and lower figures, in this case 1p. Thus the shares are valued at 381p each. If the deceased died on a Saturday or Sunday, or on a bank holiday, the figure chosen may be based on the nearest business day before or after. Surprisingly, the executor may select the date giving the most favourable valuation. Even more surprisingly, he need not, assuming there is more than one share holding, confine all the valuations to the same day, but the inventory must make it clear in every case which date is being used.

Shares in a private company or in a plc whose shares are not quoted on the stock market will require professional valuation. The basis of valuation is the price the shares would (in theory) fetch on the open market on the assumption that the prospective purchasers had available to them all the information which a prudent buyer might reasonably require if negotiating a sale by private bargain from a willing seller at arm's length. In practice, the articles of association of many private companies place restriction on the transferability of their shares, but this restriction is not taken into account in the valuation.

Government securities
Like National Savings, these are British, so they count as estate in Scotland. Government securities will normally be valued by a stockbroker on the same basis as shares in a plc, but accrued interest will either be added to or subtracted from the valuation figure. If the stock is quoted "ex div", the normal dividend will be due for payment shortly after the date of death. The apportionment of interest from date of death to date of payment is deducted from the valuation. Thus if the date of death were May 1 and payment was due on June 1, the proportion of the interest due for the month of May would be deducted. If the stock is quoted "cum div", the interest from the last payment date to date of death is added to the valuation figure. These apportionments always take place for valuation purposes even where the Apportionment Act 1870 is expressly disapplied by the will.

Unit Trusts, ISAs and PEPs
These are treated in a similar way to company shares. They can be valued by a stockbroker but the fund manager will normally do it free of charge. Approved unit trusts are not subject to the quarter-up rule. The valuation is the manager's buying back or bid price, i.e. the lower of the two figures quoted.

Income Tax
Quite frequently, a repayment of tax may be due to the deceased but the exact amount is not known. It is common professional practice to insert a notional sum, say £50.

Uncashed dividend warrants
If a dividend from shares is payable after the death of the deceased but prior to confirmation being obtained, there is a potential problem. Obviously, the payment can no longer be passed through the deceased's bank account, as it will have been frozen. The actual warrant should be returned to the company registrar with a request for the funds to be retained by the company, pending confirmation. The amount of the dividend should be shown on the inventory as an addition to the value of the shares in that particular company.

Moveable debts
Unlike the heritable debts, moveable debts are not directly deducted from the listed assets but are accounted for separately in another part of the inventory form. Thus, the global values of deceased estates, sometimes published in local newspapers, do not always reveal an entirely accurate picture. The published figure will not include heritable property passing under a special destination. Whilst the heritable property is net of debt in the inventory, the figure for moveables is gross. Thus, an estate might appear to be substantial but the moveable debts might, in fact, considerably reduce the real value.

THE OATH

Once the drafting of the inventory is complete, the executors are required to swear that, to the best of their knowledge and belief, the inventory contains a full and accurate account of the deceased's estate. If there is a will and any relevant codicils, the executors also have to swear that these are the only operative ones known to them. One executor may take the oath on behalf of all of the executors. It may be sworn before a justice of the peace, certain officials at the sheriff court or a notary public. Most solicitors are also notaries public.

SMALL ESTATES

At the time of writing, a "small" estate is one whose gross value, i.e. before deduction of debts, is not more than £30,000. This figure can be raised by statutory instrument. The small estates procedure provides a simpler option for winding up a relatively modest estate. The sheriff clerk will give assistance in completing the inventory Form C1 and there is no requirement for a separate petition for the appointment of an executor-dative, should such appointment be required. No one is obliged to use this system, if they do not wish to. The sheriff clerk himself must be satisfied that there is no competition for appointment of the executor, that the executor is the person entitled to be appointed and that the value of the gross estate does not exceed £30,000. Once the inventory is completed, the sheriff clerk is unable to provide further advice on the winding up of the estate or other legal matters.

WHERE CONFIRMATION IS NOT REQUIRED

There are occasions where confirmation is not actually required and these have already been examined in Chapter 10. In practice, where estates are very small, the need for confirmation may be waived by bodies such as government agencies and financial institutions, frequently more as a matter of privilege than of right. The general rule remains sound—that if any party pays out funds or property belonging to a deceased person to anyone other than an executor with confirmation, he does so at his own risk (*Fraser v Gibb* (1784) Mor. 3921).

SUMMARY OF THE EXECUTOR'S DUTIES

(1) He arranges for the valuation and safekeeping of the estate until such time as he can obtain confirmation. This is not the same as actually intromitting with the estate. He may consider advertising in the papers, although death is legally a public or "notorious" fact, of which notice need not be given to third parties.

(2) An executor represents the deceased, i.e. he is debtor to his creditors and creditor to his debtors.

(3) The framing of the inventory can be a major exercise but it is important to ensure it is correct as the basis for confirmation and perhaps IHT.

(4) When the inventory is framed and signed (and any IHT paid), it is lodged with the commissary office of the area in which the deceased was ordinarily resident. In the case of an executor-nominate the will, usually in extract form, is also lodged. Where there is an executor-dative, the inventory is accompanied by a bond of caution unless the applicant is a surviving spouse whose prior rights exhaust the estate.

(5) The sheriff clerk issues the confirmation, which is the executor's title to intromit with the estate. If an executor (or anyone) intromits without confirmation, his intromissions may count as vitious.

(6) If an item has been missed out of the original inventory or requires correction, a corrective inventory can be lodged and the executor will be given an eik to his original confirmation.

(7) Liability of the executor for the debts of the deceased is limited to the amount of the deceased's estate, unless he vitiously intromits.

(8) He will proceed to ingather the estate. Some items, such as bank accounts, are personal to the deceased and must be liquidated. Others, such as heritable property or stocks and shares, can be transferred to beneficiaries.

(9) He will pay preferential debts (such as deathbed and funeral expenses) as soon as possible. Ordinary debts intimated within six months of death rank *pari passu*.

(10) Eventually, he will pay the beneficiaries: special legacies first, general legacies next and residue last. Interest is payable on legacies from date to death to date of payment. Very frequently, the will provides for legacies to be paid without interest. Where interest is due, the rate is what the property or funds earned, or should have earned, if properly administered.

PAYMENT OF DEBTS

As far as creditors are concerned, the executor is the same person as the deceased (*eadem persona cum defuncto*) and is liable to the creditors to the same extent as the deceased was. However, the liability of the executor is clearly limited to the amount of the deceased's estate. If the funds in the estate are not adequate to meet the claims of all creditors in full, then some debts are regarded as privileged, e.g. funeral expenses and certain fiscal debts. When privileged debts have been paid but the remaining estate is not enough to pay the ordinary creditors in full, all claims made within six months of the death rank *pari passu*. The full order of payment of debts is set out below. Unless an executor is satisfied that the estate can meet all debts in full, he would be most unwise to pay any ordinary unsecured creditor until six months have expired from the date of death.

Even after the six month period has expired, the executor is still bound to pay any valid claim from a creditor, assuming he still has funds in hand to do so. If the executor is aware that valid debts have not been paid and he still distributes the whole estate to beneficiaries, he can find himself personally liable to pay such debts. Beneficiaries under wills frequently complain that they have to wait too long for their money. In fact, this is often due more to perception than to reality. Having paid out all debts, an executor may, a year at most after the death, start paying the beneficiaries.

Debts are basically payable in the following order—each class must be paid in full before progressing to the next class. Claimants in each class rank *pari passu.*

(1) Deathbed and funeral expenses are payable before all others, even secured debts. They cover reasonable medical expenses of the deceased's last illness as well as funeral expenses, subject again to the reasonableness test. Also included are the expenses of confirmation and the executry administration.

(2) Secured debts speak for themselves. A secured creditor is in a good position in that he can generally enforce his debt at any time. If the secured property is worth more than the debt (including interest), the creditor must account for the surplus to the estate. If the security is worth less than the debt, the creditor can rank for the deficit against the estate, but only as an ordinary creditor in respect of that proportion. A security covers any valid security granted by the deceased over his own property or implied by law, such as a landlord's hypothec.

(3) Preferred debts appear in two main categories:
    (a) Taxes and social security due, as a rule, for the 12 months prior to death; and
    (b) employees' wages for four months before death, up to a maximum of £800.

(4) Ordinary unsecured debts also speak for themselves.

(5) Inheritance tax, in practice, is paid first, often by means of a temporary overdraft, since confirmation cannot be obtained until it is paid. Nevertheless, it actually ranks last in order of priority. The point is academic; it stands to reason that if there is no estate, no IHT is payable.

If an executor believes that there is insufficient to cover the debts of the deceased, he should be advised, at an early date, to have a judicial factor or a trustee in bankruptcy appointed. If such an appointment takes place, the expenses of sequestration take precedence even over privileged debts. If an executor knows, or clearly ought to know, that an estate is insolvent and he fails to take appropriate steps, the executor's intromissions may count as vitious. In such a situation, the executor becomes personally liable for the debts of the deceased.

INCIDENCE OF DEBTS

Another matter to be addressed is what is called the "incidence" of debts. It was shown in the opening chapter that the distinction between heritable and moveable estate is still crucial in the law of succession. The question is bound to arise as to which parts of the estate are liable for which debts. The basic rule is simple: heritable debts are paid out of heritage and moveable debts out of the moveable estate. In a solvent estate, the incidence of debts is bound to affect prior rights (if the estate is intestate) and legal rights.

A debt is heritable if it is secured over heritable property. Nowadays, such a charge would be effected by a standard security recorded in the General Register of Sasines or registered in the Land Register. Other debts are paid out of moveable property, unless the will provides otherwise.

It has already been noted that problems can, and do, frequently arise when a heritable debt exists but the amount of the debt is covered by an insurance policy. Many mortgages have the capital sum covered by life assurance. Borrowers are often under the impression that, should they die during the life of the mortgage, the capital sum will automatically be repaid. It is necessary to underline the fact that a mortgage is a heritable debt and the proceeds of an insurance policy count as a moveable asset. The two do not automatically cancel one another out. A surviving spouse, under intestate succession, can take the matrimonial home (subject to the rules and limits already mentioned), but takes it subject to any existing security. Since the proceeds of the policy are moveable, these may be subject to claims for legal rights.

The matter becomes more complicated if there are two securities for the one debt. The heritable property will have been validly mortgaged to the lender by a standard security. (In the case of security granted prior to the Conveyancing and Feudal Reform (Scotland) Act 1970, this would have been effected by a bond and disposition in security or by an *ex facie* absolute disposition. These obsolete forms of security are of declining significance, but might still be encountered occasionally.) However, in some mortgages, a life insurance policy will also be formally assigned in security to the lender. To put this another way, the debt is doubly secured. In such a case, the debt must be deducted from the heritable and moveable property in proportion to the values of the two securities.

If any asset in the estate, whether heritable or moveable, is subject to a creditor's right of security, the beneficiary can only take that asset subject to the debt. In *Stewart v Stewart* (1891) 19 R. 310, a beneficiary was left the proceeds of an insurance policy. As the policy had been assigned to a creditor as security for a loan, the beneficiary was only entitled to the net proceeds.

If the will is well drafted, it may specify its own incidence of debts. So, if a house is left to a beneficiary "free of debt", then any outstanding mortgage has to be paid off out of the residue of the estate.

PARTIAL INTESTACY

As has been demonstrated, it is possible for a partial intestacy to arise. A well drafted will seeks to prevent such a possibility but, in the real world, it cannot always be avoided, especially if testators do not take the opportunity to update their wills.

It is important to notice that a surviving spouse has prior rights in the cases of partial as well as total intestacy. In the case of partial intestacy, the surviving spouse will inherit the house and furnishings (subject to the rules and limits already considered) except to the extent that these items have been disposed of by the deceased in his will (1964 Act, section 8). Also, the surviving spouse is still entitled to the financial provision of £47,000/£75,000 from the remainder of the estate which is not disposed of by will, but he must deduct from that sum the amount or value of any legacy out of the estate.

However, the surviving spouse does not have to deduct the value of a legacy of any house in which he was ordinarily resident at the time of the deceased's death. Similarly, a legacy of the furnishings of such a house does not require to be deducted (section 9(1)). If a surviving spouse decides to renounce a legacy affecting the monetary prior right, the full sum may be claimed (section 9(1)).

THE UNWORTHY HEIR

There may be certain circumstances in which an heir may be debarred from inheriting by virtue of his conduct. For many years, it was believed that, in Scotland, it was part of the common law that an unlawful killer could not benefit from his crime and thus could not inherit from the person killed. There were English cases in point, but the matter had not actually been tried in the Scottish courts. In practice, estates had been wound up on the understanding that the unlawful killer could not inherit.

The matter was first considered judicially in the sheriff court case of *Smith, Petr*, 1979 S.L.T. (Sh. Ct) 35. It was held that there was an absolute bar on inheriting if there was a conviction against the heir for murder or culpable homicide. However, the law subsequently moved on as a result of the Forfeiture Act 1982. The court was given power, at its discretion, to modify the extent of the forfeiture in the case of "unlawful killing", but not murder. In Scotland, this would mean that forfeiture could, but need not be, modified in the case of culpable homicide. In *Gilchrist, Petr*, 1990 S.L.T. 494, a wife was convicted of the culpable homicide of her husband and was admonished. The wife raised a petition seeking an order under the Act, modifying the common law rule by which she could not benefit from her own crime. It was held that, in all the circumstances of the case, an order modifying the rule in respect of 80 per cent of the estate was appropriate. Although the modification of the forfeiture is at the discretion of the court, it appears that the court does not have the discretion to modify the forfeiture entirely. In *Cross, Petr*, 1987 S.L.T. 384, the court modified the forfeiture to the extent of 100 per cent in relation to heritage and to 99 per cent in the case of moveables.

Forfeiture applies not only to property passing under a will or intestacy but also under special destinations, nominations or trusts. If an heir is disqualified because he is "unworthy", in many legal systems, his share is distributed as if he had died before the deceased. This does not seem to be the case in Scotland. In *Hunter's Exrs, Petrs*, 1992 S.L.T. 1141, Mrs H had been killed by her husband. Her will made provision for her husband, whom failing alternative beneficiaries. As Mr H had not, as a matter of fact, predeceased the alternative beneficiaries, the destination-over could not operate and the subjects of the legacy fell into intestate succession. Whilst it is difficult to fault the logic of this decision, it is unlikely that the result favoured the wishes of the testatrix.

Suicide has never been a crime in Scotland. In some cases, a life insurance policy may exclude payment where the insured voluntarily took his own life. Otherwise, there is no bar on inheriting from a suicide.

REARRANGEMENTS AFTER DEATH

Apart from a special legacy, beneficiaries have a right only to cash, not specific assets. In practice, an executor will frequently come to a private arrangement with beneficiaries as to which specific assets they might wish, such as company shares. No one is obligated to accept any legacy if he does wish to. He may disclaim a legacy or any right of succession entirely, or he may only take a proportion of his entitlement. Sometimes there may be tax advantages in rearranging the distribution of the estate and it is possible to regulate such matters by a formal deed, such as a deed of family arrangement. Any election to vary must be made within two years of the deceased's date of death and written election must be given to the Capital Taxes Office within six months of the variation. If the election involves more tax being paid by the actual executry, the executor must sign the deed as a consentor. If a formal deed was not granted, a disclaimer or election would count as a disposal for the purposes of IHT, so that additional tax would be due by the beneficiary. It is worth mentioning again that transfers of assets between spouses, whether *inter vivos* or *mortis causa*, are currently exempt from IHT.

A young person aged 16 or 17 can validly renounce legal rights or sign a deed of family arrangement. However, he might raise a subsequent challenge, up to the age of 21, that doing so had caused him substantial prejudice. It would certainly be prudent for an executor to seek judicial ratification of the discharge or variation under section 4 of the Age of Legal Capacity (Scotland) Act 1991.

DISCHARGE OF EXECUTORS

In their own interests, executors should normally seek formal discharge at the close of their administration. The matter of discharge is considered further in the next chapter.

---

13. TRUSTS

Trusts, in one form or another, have been with us for centuries and remain an important part of private law. Trusts were particularly popular with the Victorians, but have been adapted to a wide variety of modern uses. Trusts can just as easily arise *inter vivos* as *mortis causa*. In this final chapter, only the latter will be considered in any detail.

As the name suggests, this area is based first and foremost on trust rather than law. One party entrusts property and duties to another and, in so doing, relies on his honesty, fair play and obedience to instructions. In former times, trusts were largely governed by common law, but there were considerable statutory inroads made in the 19th century. The main governing statutes are now the Trusts (Scotland) Acts of 1921 (the "1921 Act") and 1961 (the "1961 Act"). The common law does, however, still have an important role.

Since executors are trustees by statutory definition, there is considerable overlap between the law of trusts and of succession. Nevertheless, there are distinctions. The executor obtains confirmation, ingathers the estate, pays the debts and then distributes. At that point, the executor's duties are at an end. If there are continuing trust purposes, the administration of these begins when property or funds are transferred to the trustees. Even if (as is common) the executors and trustees are the same individuals, their two roles are separate.

CONSTITUTION

Ideally, a trust should be constituted expressly, although no technical wording is required, only a clear intention to set up a trust. If the trust is testamentary, writing is an absolute requirement, as in the case of any bequest.

A trustee has legal title to the property and effectively owns it, but his title is not beneficial to himself. Persons who receive the benefit, i.e. the beneficiaries, whether of property, capital or income have the beneficial interest or *jus crediti* (right to the benefit).

There are two other requirements for a valid trust, both of which are fairly obvious. There must be actual property, heritable or moveable, and there must be some purpose for this property being held by trustees. The purpose may, in practice, be very simple, such as holding property until a beneficiary attains a particular age.

A *mortis causa* trust can only be created by a testamentary writing, normally a trust disposition and settlement ("TD and S"). Such a trust does not come into effect until the death of the truster. As long as the truster is living and competent, he can revoke the testamentary writing. If the purposes of a *mortis causa* trust fail or do not exhaust the estate, the surplus property can be claimed by those entitled by succession, e.g. a residuary legatee or heirs in intestacy.

PUBLIC AND PRIVATE TRUSTS

Every trust will be either private or public. In practice, the majority of trusts are private. In a private trust, the beneficiaries will always be private individuals, either expressly named or easily identified as a private class, e.g. "my nephews". Only beneficiaries or others with a direct interest have any title to sue. If a private *mortis causa* trust fails before it even comes into effect, the property will revert to the deceased's estate.

There are provisions for variation of the purposes of a private trust once it has come into operation. The common law possibilities for variation were limited and, in any event, required the consent of all beneficiaries. The 1961 Act brought in reasonably wide powers to allow either the beneficiaries or the trustees to petition for variation of its terms or purposes. The common law position whereby all beneficiaries (including potential beneficiaries) must consent is retained. However, provided the court is satisfied that relevant interests are not being prejudiced, it may consent on behalf of one or more of them. This provision included a beneficiary of non-age or other incapacity, a potential future beneficiary and any person unborn. The court must be satisfied that such implied consent is not prejudicial to the beneficiaries, or potential beneficiaries, concerned. The Court of Session has considerable powers to approve an arrangement varying or revoking any of the trust purposes or to enlarge the given powers of trustees.

One fairly obvious reason for varying the provisions of a private trust is the mitigation of tax liability. In *Colville, Petr*, 1962 S.C. 185, it was held that this was a proper use of the 1961 Act provisions. The court may also revoke an alimentary liferent as long as it is satisfied that the arrangement is reasonable, taking account of the beneficiary's other income and all the circumstances of the case. As indicated in Chapter 6, at common law an alimentary liferent could not be revoked once it was operational, although it could be revoked before it actually commenced.

A public trust, as the name would suggest, is for the benefit of the public, or a proportion or class of the public. Normally, such a trust will be of an educational, religious or charitable nature, or a mixture. The fact that such trusts are public has nothing to do with their size. Some public trusts are small, although the Law Reform (Miscellaneous Provisions) (Scotland) Act 1990 first opened the way to amalgamation or disbursement of certain small and outdated public trusts. Many, but not all, public trusts are also charitable. The Charities and Trustee Investment (Scotland) Act 2005 (the "2005 Act") introduced major changes to the law affecting charities in Scotland, setting up, for the first time, the Office of the Scottish Charity Regulator (the "OSCR"). There is now a public register of charities and the OSCR has wide powers to monitor, investigate and take action to ensure good practice and protect assets where appropriate. The 2005 Act (section 7) also provides statutory definitions of what are recognised as charitable purposes.

In the case of a public trust, any member of the public having an interest to do so has a title to sue. Occasionally, there has been doubt as to whether a particular trust is public or private. In

Salvesen's Trs v Wye, 1954 S.C. 440, there was a legacy to "poor relatives, friends or acquaintances". The court held that the beneficiaries' connection with the testator was the dominant factor rather than their poverty and, accordingly, it was a private trust. On the other hand, in the older case of *Andrews v Ewart's Trs* (1886) 13 R. (HL) 69, a trust set up for the establishment of a school was held to be a public trust and title to sue rested with members of the public who might wish to avail themselves of this educational provision.

The major difference from a private trust was traditionally found in the mechanism for changing the purposes of an existing trust. If public trust purposes fail, the trustees may petition the Court of Session to ask it, under its *nobile officium,* to approve a *cy-près* (pronounced "see pray") scheme, i.e. to rearrange or reorganise the trust as closely as possible to the original directions. If, however, the truster had expressed a clear intention only to benefit one restricted purpose or a particular institution (i.e. no general public purpose can be implied) a *cy-près* scheme is not appropriate and the trust purposes would fail from the beginning. In *Burgess' Trs v Crawford*, 1912 S.C. 387, a bequest provided for the establishment of an industrial school for females. Due to a change in the law, it was impossible to carry out these directions. The bequest lapsed entirely as no other public or charitable purpose was stated or implied, so *cy-près* was inappropriate.

In strict theory, a *cy-près* scheme will not be approved unless the original purposes are impossible (not merely difficult) or are ludicrous, although this principle has not always been slavishly followed by the Court of Session.

The 1990 Act broadened the law by providing (section 9) that where it is no longer possible for trustees to carry out the trust purposes in the manner prescribed, the court may approve a statutory reorganisation. This may take place where, having regard to social or economic changes, the trust purposes are obsolete or lacking in usefulness.

The 1990 Act also contains provisions for dealing with other problems in the administration of smaller public trusts, allowing very small trusts to amalgamate or wind up their affairs and transfer funds to another charity, under the supervision of the court.

The 2005 Act does not repeal the provisions of the 1990 Act, but it introduces a regime under which the OSCR will be able to oversee amalgamations and reorganisations of charitable trusts.

TRUSTEES

At the heart of the common law of trusts is the concept of property vesting in trustees. A trustee is the legal owner of the property, but his ownership is not beneficial. He owns it in order to administer it on behalf of the beneficiaries. Trustees under the 1921 Act (section 2) include not only trustees appointed by a deed of trust, but also trustees *ex officio*, executors and judicial factors. However, the common law also applies to any person in a position of trust, such as a company director, a partner on behalf of his firm or an agent on behalf of his principal. The late Professor Andrew Dewar Gibb, somewhat whimsically, defined a trustee as "a person who is animated either by extreme good will towards the person who made him a trustee or by a light hearted ignorance of what he is undertaking" (*A Preface to Scots Law*, 3rd edn, 1961, p.28). Although normally a trustee carries out his duties gratuitously, the responsibilities are onerous and the courts tend to be fairly strict in the area of enforcement. No one can be compelled to accept the office of a trustee. No specific form of consent to acting as a trustee is insisted upon by law, but writing is clearly desirable, especially in the case of someone being appointed (assumed) to an existing trust.

The 2005 Act introduces a new form of trustee, the charity trustee, who now has clear statutory duties and for whom mis-management can also be interpreted as misconduct.

DUTIES OF TRUSTEES

The actual duties of trustees are largely governed by common law although certain trustees, such as charity trustees, are governed by statutory provisions. It is obvious that a trustee must administer the trust estate in line with the directions of the truster. In many ways, the common law duties of a trustee are similar to that of an executor, but not identical.

(1) A trustee must ingather, administer and distribute the estate. Frequently, in a *mortis causa* trust, the trustees and executors are the same individuals. If a testator appoints trustees but fails to provide for executors, the trustees are entitled to be appointed as executors (Executors (Scotland) Act 1900, section 3). This is more likely to arise in a home-made TD and S.

(2) Trustees are under a general duty to complete title to property which forms part of the trust estate.

(3) A trustee is expected to exercise due care. The standard of care is that of a reasonably prudent person in the management of his own affairs. What a trustee's own personal standards are in the care of his own property is of no consequence. If a trustee fails to meet a reasonable standard, he may lay himself open personally to an action for damages.

(4) The office of trustee is essentially one of *delectus personae* (choice of person) and demands his personal attention. He cannot delegate his ultimate responsibility to another party, no matter how skilled that party might be. This does not mean that a trustee cannot take professional advice. There are times where this is clearly wise and prudent. Advice should be written and come from a person who is reasonably believed by the trustees to be qualified to give it. However, at the end of the day, trustees must take the responsibility of decision. It is wise, in practice, to keep records not only of what the decisions of the trustees were but also why they were made. The 2005 Act allows trustees to select nominees and also allows trustees to delegate investment and management of funds where the trust deed is silent.

(5) One particularly important duty of a trustee is, in fact, a negative one, not to be *auctor in rem suam* (one who acts in his own interest). This means that a trustee's interests as an individual must not, even potentially, be brought into conflict with his duties as a trustee, since these duties are fiduciary. This principle is so strictly applied that the question as to whether or not any conflicting contract was fair or unfair is not taken into account. The rule applies not only to trustees in the narrower sense but also to agents, guardians, company directors, partners and anyone whose position is fiduciary. The most famous case on conflict of interest must be *Aberdeen Railway Company v Blaikie Bros* (1853) 1 Macq. 461, involving Sir Thomas Blaikie, sometime Lord Provost of Aberdeen. Blaikie, the managing partner of Blaikie Bros, iron founders in Aberdeen, was also a director of the Aberdeen Railway Company. Blaikie Bros brought an action against the railway company for implement of a contract in which the latter had agreed to purchase a large quantity of iron materials. In the House of Lords, the original contract was declared to be voidable. Blaikie, as a director of the railway company, was in a position of trust and was thus precluded from entering into a contract on its behalf with a firm of which he was himself a partner. It was not suggested, nor implied, that he had acted fraudulently. In *Cherry's Trs v Patrick*, 1911 S.L.T. 313, a trustee was a supplier of alcoholic liquor. He made certain profits by trading with public houses forming part of the trust estate. It was held that these profits could not be retained by him but must be accounted for to the trust estate. In *Clark v Clark's Exrs*, 1989 S.L.T. 665, executors agreed to sell heritable property forming part of the executry estate to a third party. The third party then agreed to convey the property to one of the executors in her personal capacity. As this executor was clearly *auctor in rem suam*, the sale was reduced.

(6) The office of trustee is gratuitous and no trustee has the right to be paid for his work, however skilled or arduous, unless

there is express power to do so in the trust deed. Payment includes commission. A trustee would be able to transact with the trust or the beneficiaries if such transactions were authorised by the truster or the beneficiaries, in full knowledge of their rights. The burden of proof would be on the trustee to show that he had acted in a fair and honest manner and that full information and value had been given. If a trustee gains some personal benefit by being a trustee, he must declare it, since such benefit is really held on constructive trust for the beneficiaries.

(7) It is not surprising that trustees must keep proper and adequate records of their intromissions both with capital and income.

(8) Common law and statute law come together in a particularly important duty, to keep the trust funds properly invested. The trust deed itself will frequently give wide powers to trustees or give fairly specific directions. At common law and in the absence of directions, trustees were restricted to certain fixed interest securities, feu duties, ground annuals and heritable securities. Even if a truster directs that certain investments are to be retained, it seems that the trustees are under a duty to ensure that such investments continue to be in the best interests of the beneficiaries, even if that means disposing of investments and reinvesting the proceeds (*Thomson's Trs v Davidson*, 1947 S.C. 654).

Where there were no directions given in the trust deed (which would be unusual in a professionally drafted document) the Trustee Investment Act 1961 used to apply. This Act was intended to widen significantly the investment powers of trustees. In practice its provisions were found to be administratively irksome and it was repealed by the 2005 Act. Under the 2005 Act (Part 3) trustees generally have the same powers of investment as if they were beneficial owners. This includes power to invest in heritable property. These provisions apply to all trustees, not just charity trustees. The fact that the trustees have taken advice does not relieve them of their basic duty of care. Their overarching duty in investment is to secure the best possible return to the trust.

POWERS OF TRUSTEES

Obviously, the first place to look is the trust deed. Where the deed is silent, the trustees have powers implied by both common law and statute. The Court of Session may also exercise its *nobile officium* to give further powers to the trustees where the trust is unworkable.

The most basic common law power of trustees is to administer the trust on a day to day basis. The 1921 and 1961 Acts set out

certain powers, provided they are not at variance with the provisions of the trust deed. These include the power to sell the estate,
to grant leases, borrow money on the security of the estate, appoint
agents and solicitors and grant all necessary deeds.

Unless there is only one trustee, the right to exercise the powers
belongs to the majority of the surviving and accepting trustees. All
trustees must be given the full opportunity to attend meetings and
to participate in the administration of the trust. Sometimes, the
deed of trust itself may provide for a *quorum*. In the absence of
such a provision, the 1921 Act provides that a majority of accepting
and surviving trustees is a valid *quorum*.

Under section 2 of the 1961 Act, the validity of the sale by
trustees of heritable property to a third party may not be challenged on the ground that such sale is contrary to the terms of the
trust, provided the third party acted in good faith and for value.
Thus anyone buying heritable property from trustees does not
require to satisfy himself that they have power to sell, unless there
is anything to put him on his guard. The section 2 provision does
not affect the relationship between the trustees and the beneficiaries. Thus, even although trustees can grant a valid title to a third
party when, in fact, they have no power to sell, they open
themselves to an action for damages on the grounds of breach of
trust at the hands of an aggrieved beneficiary. If the third party had
not acted in good faith, the beneficiary would be able to follow the
particular investment and reclaim it.

LIABILITY OF TRUSTEES

Trustees are not liable for the truster's debts beyond the value of
the estate at their disposal. If trustees or executors discover that
the inherited debts exceed the value of the estate, in their own
interests they should take steps to have the estate sequestrated. If
they do not take this possibly painful step, their own intromissions
may count as vitious, leaving them with personal liability for the
debts of the deceased.

It is often, quite wrongly, assumed that trustees incur no
personal liability for debts incurred in their administration of the
trust. This is not so as, basically, a testamentary trust does not have
a distinct personality in law. Most trusts are unincorporated bodies,
although public trusts and charities are increasingly incorporated as
companies limited by guarantee. Subject to that exception, trustees
are personally liable, jointly and severally, for the debts they incur
in the course of their administration. However, they are entitled to
reimbursement in full from the trust estate, provided the debts

have been properly incurred. In most cases, this personal liability does not cause problems. The result would be otherwise if the assets of the trust estate were insufficient to cover the debts. In *Muir v City of Glasgow Bank* (1879) 6 R. (HL) 21, a shareholder died, leaving his estate in trust. Among the trust assets was stock in the City of Glasgow Bank, an unlimited company. The stock was transferred into the names of his two children as trustees. The Bank crashed in 1878, leaving its shareholders with unlimited liability for its vast debts. Only 254 of its 1,819 shareholders remained solvent. The two trustees argued that their liability was limited to the extent of the trust estate. The House of Lords held that they were personally liable to meet all legitimate calls in full.

A trustee who is in breach of trust may well have to pay back all the loss this breach has caused to the trust estate. "Breach" can cover a wide variety of omissions and commissions, from fraud to negligence and in varying degrees. It would be breach of trust to fail to make proper provisions for investment of funds or to delay unreasonably in paying beneficiaries. As stated above, trustees have joint and several liability, although breach by one trustee, without the knowledge or acquiescence of the others, does not make them liable if they have acted reasonably.

It is not unusual for a trust deed to include an indemnity clause stating that the trustees are not to be held personally liable for omissions, error or neglect. The courts have tended to interpret such clauses restrictively and have not allowed them to protect a trustee who is blatantly in breach of duty, as in *Knox v Mackinnon* (1888) 15 R. (HL) 83.

ASSUMPTION, RESIGNATION AND REMOVAL OF TRUSTEES

Unless the trust deed provides to the contrary, new trustees can be appointed or assumed by existing trustees. From the practical point of view, such assumptions would normally be in writing and the 1921 Act provides appropriate styles. If there are two existing trustees, both must sign the deed of assumption. If there are more than two, a *quorum* is sufficient but, in practice, the signature of all trustees is desirable.

Although an executor-dative counts as a trustee with the same rights as a gratuitous trustee at common law and under the 1921 and 1961 Acts, he does not have the right of assumption (Succession (Scotland) Act 1964, section 20). If there are no surviving trustees, the court may make an appointment or may appoint a judicial factor to administer the estate.

At common law a trustee had no power to resign but, under the 1921 Act, is entitled to do so, subject to important exceptions:

(1) A sole trustee cannot resign unless he has assumed new accepting trustees or the court has either appointed new trustees or a judicial factor.
(2) If a trustee accepts office on condition of a legacy or remuneration, he will require the permission of the court to resign and he may be required to make appropriate repayment.
(3) An executor-dative has no power to resign.

For his own protection, a resigning trustee should execute a formal minute of resignation to avoid any possible personal liability for the future acts of his co-trustees. Frequently such a minute is incorporated into a deed of assumption of a new trustee. It is good practice to register such a document in the Books of Council and Session. The court will normally, as a matter of course, remove a trustee on the grounds of insanity, disability, absence or disappearance. Whilst the court has the general power to remove a trustee on such grounds as gross negligence, wilful breach of trust or fraud, this is a power which, historically, has been used only sparingly. Generally, the courts are reluctant to remove a trustee who has been acting in good faith even if his interpretation or administration has fallen short. If there is a deadlock among trustees, the courts may appoint a judicial factor, which will suspend the powers of trustees for as long as his appointment lasts.

RESTRICTIONS ON TRUST PURPOSES

There are restrictions on the purposes for which a trust may be constituted both under common law and statute law. These are, to all intents and purposes, identical to those applying to testamentary provisions, covered in Chapter 6.

JUDICIAL FACTORS

A judicial factor ("JF") is really a special kind of trustee. At one time a JF was appointed only by the Court of Session under its *nobile officium*, but the right of appointment is now well established in the sheriff court. Although a JF is a trustee within the meaning of the 1921 Act, in essence he is an official of the court whose rights and duties are regulated by statute.

A JF is appointed by and answerable only to the court. He always functions on his own and is only permitted to resign from office with the authority of the court. A JF must find caution, usually a bond provided by an insurance company. The person whose funds are in his care is called the "ward".

The very basic function of a JF is to look after estates where some element of protection is required or a degree of fair play has to be ensured. Examples relevant to this area of law would be where trustees are in deadlock or where all original or assumed trustees have died. The court will appoint a JF as a result of a petition stating the grounds, the property to be taken into his charge and the name of the person to be appointed. An interim appointment may be obtained in the case of urgency.

The JF's authority to intromit with the estate is the extract decree of appointment which has a similar effect to an executor's confirmation. Unlike most trustees, a JF would not normally complete title to the property of the ward but has power to intromit with the estate in the ward's name, under the general superintendence of the Accountant of Court. However, normally a JF has all the general powers of a trustee, although, as shown in Chapter 11, he is unable to exercise dispositive discretion.

TERMINATION OF TRUSTS

Traditionally, English law has considerable suspicion of anything that appears to make a trust perpetual. In Scotland, we tend not to see this as such a great problem. There are trusts that have existed in Scotland for generations and are still in good heart. Nevertheless, most trusts come to an end sooner or later. In a *mortis causa* trust the testator can validly revoke the provisions in the TD and S at any time up to his death.

Trustees can normally only terminate a trust by administering the trust according to its stated purposes and making a final and total distribution (denuding) in favour of the beneficiaries. If the trust assets were distributed to the wrong beneficiaries, the trust would not be at an end even though the trustees had denuded. It is a trustee's nightmare to make a major mistake in the disbursement of assets by, say, paying the wrong beneficiary or overpaying the correct one. It used to be thought that, as a very general rule of thumb, if a wrong payment was made due to an error of fact, it could be recovered, but not so if there was an error of law. In the Inner House case of *Morgan Guaranty Trust Company of New York v Lothian Regional Council*, 1995 S.L.T. 299, a Bench of five judges effectively abolished the error of law rule.

Trustees have a particularly high duty in identifying the correct beneficiaries. If trustees make a payment to the wrong beneficiary, this potentially attracts personal liability. However, under the Law Reform (Miscellaneous Provisions) (Scotland) Act 1968, section 7, trustees were not under a duty to enquire about possible illegitimate relatives of the testator, unless they were put on their guard that such might exist. It has been demonstrated that the status of illegitimacy has now finally been abolished.

Beneficiaries have very limited powers to request termination of a trust. Potentially, it is possible, provided they all consent and it does not prejudice the trustees in their proper administration or interfere with any alimentary rights. As demonstrated in Chapter 6, a beneficiary may also request termination where the remaining trust purposes are only of an administrative nature and the beneficiary has a full vested right of fee (*Miller's Trs v Miller* (1890) 18 R. 301).

DISCHARGE OF TRUSTEES

It is common sense for trustees to ask for a discharge before a final distribution is made to beneficiaries so as to avoid any future personal liability. Normally trustees will not denude until a discharge has been granted but, once it has been granted, they are bound to do so. To put it another way, a trust is not really at an end until the trustees are discharged.

The discharge can only cover what is within the knowledge of the party granting it. If a beneficiary grants a discharge unaware that a trustee has carried out a major fraud, he could still bring a challenge at a later date when the facts come to light. If, however, a beneficiary was aware that a breach of trust had taken place yet signed a discharge he would be personally barred from founding on the breach at a later date.

Whilst each individual trustee is entitled to a discharge, one discharge in favour of all trustees is common. The trust deed itself may lay down the actual format of the discharge, in which case the instructions will be followed. Since the Requirements of Writing (Scotland) Act 1995 came into effect, a document is formally valid if subscribed by the granter. Accordingly, a simple signature on a discharge is adequate but it is common practice for the discharge to be self proving and for it to be registered in the Books of Council and Session. The strict legal effect of granting a discharge is to protect trustees from future liability under the trust and to close off any challenge to their intromissions. This does not mean that trustees who have been discharged are beyond all possible challenge. The correct approach would be for the aggrieved party to raise an action of reduction in respect of the discharge, e.g. that

it was granted as a result of fraud, essential error or breach of trust.
Such actions in respect of trustees are, fortunately, rare in practice.

APPENDIX 1: SAMPLE EXAMINATION QUESTIONS AND ANSWER PLANS

GENERAL COMMENTS

It is neither hinted nor suggested that the outline answers which
follow the questions are some model of perfection. Everyone has
his or her own form of expression, but some basic comments may
be helpful.

(1) The examiner is a person working under pressure. He has to
read and assess many scripts in a short period of time, whilst
attempting to remain scrupulously fair. His task will be made easier
if your response is both tidy and succinct. Note carefully the
number of marks given for each part of a question. This should
give guidance as to how long you can afford to take. If you write a
very long answer for a 5 mark question, you are wasting your
resources.

(2) There is no harm in making rough notes and drafts. There is
a universal concordat among examiners that they ignore anything
that has a line drawn through it. They have better things to do than
to read your rough notes and possible mistakes as well as your
main text.

(3) Lawyers—and examiners—look for authority and precedent.
Avoid, like the plague, the expression "I think". The important
factor is not what you may happen to think, so much as what you
deduce or conclude. Your opinion is obviously relevant, but why
and how have you formed it? Have you, for example, a case or
statute in point? Examiners like cases.

(4) If you remember a relevant case, but cannot remember the
names of the parties, do still use the case. It is far better to say "in
a settled case" or "in *A v B*" rather than miss it out. Remember
that the examiner is looking to see if he can pass candidates, not
for ways to fail them. You need to put all your goods in the shop
window, including those that are not quite perfect. Examiners are
always more generous with their first 50 marks than their second
50, but they can only judge what you put on the paper. Try not to

be too long-winded when applying cases. You do not need to lovingly give out each factual detail. By all means give a very brief summary of relevant facts but make sure you apply the *ratio* of the case. Many students think they have used a case by simply reciting the facts, but without applying them. Equally annoying to an examiner is when as candidate writes "See the case of. . ." without giving any kind of explanation or application. This name dropping is of no value and may well be counter-productive.

(5) Assume, when answering, that the person who is reading your answer is intelligent and quick on the uptake but has little or no previous knowledge of the subject. Does your answer give a sufficiently clear explanation?

(6) It is part of legal training to see both sides of any question. Do not be afraid, however, to express a concluding opinion where the question is a legal problem. Of course, you must put all sides of the argument into your answer; but it will not do to leave your answer so open-ended that you appear to be inviting the examiner to choose the correct conclusion for you.

SAMPLE QUESTIONS WITH ANSWERS

(1)(a) Give a detailed explanation of a widow's housing right under the prior rights applicable on intestacy.
(b) If the deceased owned two homes, what effect does this have on the financial provision available to the widow under prior rights?
(c) You are the second of two children of the third of four brothers of your Aunt Matilda. She is survived by three sisters and all her brothers (apart from your father); she is also survived by her elderly widowed mother. The total net value of her estate is £56,000, of which £50,000 is heritable and £6,000 is moveable. Giving reasons for your answer, how much are you due from Matilda's estate?

(a) Housing right in intestacy
This is a straightforward question on substantive law, as it affects prior rights. Under the 1964 Act a surviving spouse is entitled to the ownership or tenancy of any one house owned or tenanted by the deceased at the time of his death. What is crucial to remember is that the *surviving spouse* must have been ordinarily resident in the house in question at the time of the intestate's death. It is not a requirement that the intestate himself was ordinarily resident.

At present, the maximum value of this benefit is £300,000. (Check that this figure is up to date.) If the interest of the deceased exceeds that figure, the surviving spouse is entitled to a sum of £300,000 only. The survivor takes the property subject to any existing secured loan. Frequently, the deceased may only have owned a one half *pro indiviso* share in the property, due to its being held in joint names of the spouses. In that case, the survivor takes the half share, up to a value of £300,000. If the title was taken subject to a special destination, the half share passes automatically to the survivor and is not confirmed to. In such a case, there would be no dwelling house right to be claimed.

If the house forms part of subjects included with a tenancy or where it forms part of subjects used by the deceased for the purposes of a trade, profession or occupation, a cash sum would normally be paid. If the deceased owned more than one house *and* the survivor was ordinarily resident in both of them at the time of his death, she has a period of six months to elect which one to take. Perhaps it is worth underlining, in closing, that prior rights only apply in intestacy and apply equally to widows and widowers (and, of course, now to civil partners).

(b) Apportionment of financial provision between heritable and moveable

After the dwelling house and furniture rights have been satisfied, the survivor is entitled to the sum of £75,000, or £42,000 if there are surviving children and/or representatives. (Again, check that these figures are up to date.) If there is both heritable and moveable property in the estate after satisfaction of the dwelling house and furniture rights (as there would be in this case, because there is a second house), the financial provision is paid proportionately out of both heritable and moveable estate.

(c) Problem question

This is the sort of question that may fluster candidates in the heat of the moment. If in doubt, draw a family tree. You can always draw your pen through it after you have attempted the question.

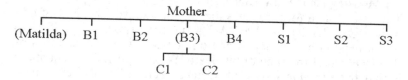

In other words, you are C2. Since Matilda died intestate without spouse or children, her entire estate counts as dead's part. According to the rules of division, the dead's part would first be divided into two half-shares, one going to the mother and the other being divided along the collateral line. In the latter case, representation applies. The fact that the estate is a mixture of heritable and moveable property is no more than a distraction since the division of dead's part does not differentiate between the two. Accordingly, £28,000 is available for distribution along the collateral line. B3 has predeceased leaving two children to represent. Since all the claimants are not in the same degree of relationship to the deceased, the division will be *per stirpes*. Those who are nearest to the deceased are obviously her brothers and sisters; the branches will be from that generation, giving seven in all. Each branch is worth £4,000; B1, B2, B4, S1, S2 and S3 can take an entire branch, but B3's branch will be shared between C1 and C2. As C2, your share is £2,000.

(2) (a) In which circumstances may conditions attached to a legacy be set aside and the legacy paid notwithstanding?
(b) What are the effects on other claimants of a child discharging any claim to legitim (1) before and (2) after the death of his parent?
(c) George dies leaving net estate of £195,000. In his will he directs that his house (value £150,000) is to be sold and the proceeds shared between Gladys, a young lady with whom he has been having a passionate affair, and the benevolent fund of his former army regiment. His moveable estate is valued at £45,000 and is left in entirety to Gladys. George's wife, Clarinda, went back to live with her mother 10 years ago, but there was no divorce or judicial separation. Their twin sons, Bill and Ben, live with George, as does George's widowed mother who has kept house since Clarinda went back to her mother. Clarinda, Bill, Ben and George's mother all are angry and affronted at George's will and determined to press for every last penny to which they are entitled. Assuming that George was sane when he made his will and that it was validly executed, how much—if anything—might each claimant get? Give a brief explanation to justify your conclusions.

(a) Setting aside conditions in a will
You would have to gauge carefully how many marks are assigned to this question so as to ensure that you do not get carried away and write far more than the question is worth. The classic examples are:

(1) Void conditions, where a condition is set aside on the grounds that it is uncertain, illegal, immoral or contrary to public policy. There is more than adequate case law in Chapters 6 and 11. If the condition is set aside, the legacy can be paid, without "strings attached". If, however, there is no obvious beneficiary, as in the cases of the eccentric McCaig family or the Musselburgh butcher, the entire legacy provision will fail.

(2) Repugnancy, where conditions attached to a legacy are inconsistent with the main tenor of the legacy itself. One example would be where a legacy is given in full fee, but trustees are then directed to hold the capital and pay only the revenue to the beneficiary. The direction to the trustees would be repugnant and the beneficiary would receive the full fee.

(3) Accumulation of income (as a rule of thumb) for more than 21 years after the death of a testator. Be careful again not to wax too lyrical on *Thelluson v Woodford* (1799) or *Elder's Trs v Free Church of Scotland* (1892) if there are only a few marks allocated to this question. It is perfectly legitimate to accumulate for up to 21 years and whatever is "in the bag" is there legitimately. After the 21 years are past, the surplus income must be distributed to those who would have been entitled if accumulation had not been directed in the first place.

(4) Liferents created in favour of parties not yet born. The Law Reform (Miscellaneous Provisions) (Scotland) Act 1968 provides that it is not possible to create a liferent in favour of someone who is not alive or *in utero* at the date of the creator's death. If a testator attempts to do so, the liferent property will belong absolutely to the beneficiary at the date when he becomes entitled to the liferent, provided he is aged 18; if he is under that age, he must wait until attaining the age of 18.

(b) Discharge of legitim

A good, classic question, although few people actually do want to discharge legal rights before the death of a parent. The first point to make is crucial: the legitim fund is fixed as at date of death and (leaving aside payment of interest on the principal sum) does not increase or decrease in value. The actual value of the fund is not affected by discharge of legitim before or after the parent's death. However, the potential difference in the effect on other claimants, i.e. siblings or their representatives, is substantial. If a child renounces his legal rights before the death of his parent he is deemed (for this purpose only) to have died before his parent and to have left no issue to represent (even if the true situation is different). The result is that the amount available to other claimants is bound to be more. If there are three children, for example, and one has predeceased leaving no issue, the legitim fund will be divided in two rather than in three. Any renunciation of legal rights before the death of a parent would have to be express; it could not be implied.

If the renunciation takes place after the death of the parent, the effect is different. Because legal rights are fixed at the moment of the parents's death, nothing that takes place after that death can change the amounts designated for each claimant. Thus the portion of the legitim funds which has been renounced falls into dead's part or residue, as the case may be. So, if there are three children, one of whom renounces legal rights after the death of his parent, his two siblings can still only claim one third of the legitim fund each, the remaining third going to dead's part or residue. A discharge of legal rights after the death of the parent could be express or it could be implied since the acceptance of a legacy provision, whether of heritable or moveable estate, is deemed to be in full and final settlement of legal rights unless (unlikely) the will expressly states otherwise.

(c) Problem

This is a good question and only slightly larger than life. Starting with the heritable property, there is no member of the family who can prevent George disposing of it. A widow's dwellinghouse right only applies in intestacy and she must have been ordinarily resident in the house in question. Clarinda fails on both counts. The fact that George directs his house to be sold does not alter the fact that the property was heritable at the time of his death. However, Clarinda can claim legal rights, i.e. relict's part, and the children can claim legitim out of the moveable estate. Unfortunately, the widowed mother has no claim, as only legal rights can prevail against a will. Thus Clarinda can claim £15,000 (one third of the net moveable estate) and the children share the legitim fund of £15,000 between them. Assuming that the house is sold for its exact valuation figure, the final distribution would be as follows:

		£
GLADYS—half share of house		75,000
	residue	15,000
BENEVOLENT FUND -half share of house		75,000
CLARINDA—relict's part		15,000
BILL—share of legitim		7,500
BEN—share of legitim		7,500
MOTHER		Nil
		195,000

(3) (a) Mr Grimm is a widower in his seventies. Although not rich, Mr Grimm is quite comfortable, owning his house outright, a car, a considerable portfolio of shares and some interesting paintings. In addition, he has some items of jewellery which belonged to his late wife and which are expected to appreciate considerably in the near

future. Grimm's only relatives are his two sons, one of whom is very close to him, but the other is the "black sheep" of the family. Grimm wants to make a testamentary provision which will favour the one son and exclude the other—at least as far as this is possible.

(b) The late John, a bachelor, was the middle of five children, with two older sisters and two younger brothers. Only John's younger brother, George, married; this brother had two children but died before John. The other brother and the two sisters survived John; their parents both died many years ago. George's widow alleges that John signed a will leaving his estate to be shared equally among his brothers and sisters and thus, she claims, she is entitled to a share. Explain the effect of (1) John having left such a will and (2) John having died intestate.

(a) The exclusion of the "black sheep"

You would point out to G that if he dies testate, the only claim which either of his sons could make against his estate is that of legal rights. Children can claim against a notional legitim fund which is either a one half-share of the net moveable estate where there is no surviving spouse (as in this case) or a one third-share where there is a surviving spouse. Thus even if G tries to exclude his wayward son from the succession, he cannot do so, as the son can claim (in this case) one quarter of his net moveable estate in spite of what the will states. All Grimm can actually do is to minimise the extent of his moveable estate. He could give a substantial amount, such as the jewellery, to his favourite son here and now—although this attracts a potential inheritance tax liability. Another possibility is the conversion of as much of his moveable property as possible into actual heritage.

(b) The family problem

Plenty of potential here for family disagreement and ill feeling! Obviously, we do not know all the facts but it is worth pointing out briefly that where it is known that a person made a will but, at the time of his death, it cannot be found, the presumption is that the deceased destroyed that will *animo revocandi*.

(1) John did leave such a will

The first matter to dispose of is George's widow's claim. Unless the will expressly provided for her, she could not take any share in place of George, since George had died before his brother and it is a basic rule of succession that a legatee must survive the deceased in order to acquire a vested right. However, another question arises: what happens to George's notional share of the estate? Does it automatically accresce to the siblings or does it fall into the residue or even into intestacy? It is worth underlining that the first place to look is the actual will in the hope that precise instructions are set out there. If they are not, the basic presumptions apply but even these will differ according to the wording of the will. If a legacy is joint, "to X and Y", there will be accretion. So, if X dies before the testator, his share accresces to that of Y. However, if there are words of severance, such as "share and share alike", there is a presumption against accretion, unless the legacy is to a class of persons, such as "my brothers and sisters". There is further complication that if the members of the class are specifically named, there is a presumption against accretion.

(2) John having died intestate

If John was intestate, his entire estate would have to be dealt with as dead's part, since there is no surviving spouse and no children. The estate will be shared out among the class making up his brothers and sisters. Whilst there is representation in respect of the dead's part, that representation is only in favour of descendants and not to a spouse of the predeceasing claimant. Thus if George left children, they could represent their father and claim his share *per stirpes*. If there are no children or descendants of George, the estate will be divided *per capita* among the surviving brother and the two sisters.

(4) (a) The will of the late Kate leaves her nephew Cuthbert the heritable property known as Claybogs Farm. It has always been Cuthbert's wish and expectation to own and farm that property and his aunt had acquainted him with the contents of her will some time ago. Very shortly before her death, Kate sold the farm for £400,000. The proceeds of the sale are still in the hands of her solicitor. Cuthbert is disappointed that the farm has been sold but is looking forward to receiving £400,000 instead. Advise Cuthbert.

(b) Augustus has no relatives, so he leaves his house and a portfolio of shares worth £50,000 to Bill (a friend) whom failing to Freda (another friend). Bill, a bachelor, enjoys ownership of the house and shares for a few months but then dies unexpectedly. Freda is wondering if the house and shares will now come to her. Advise Freda.

(a) Great expectations

It looks as though Cuthbert's great expectations are about to be dashed. It may well be that Aunt Kate had intended to leave him the money instead of the farm. Unfortunately, she did not change her will and, where a will is perfectly clear and unambiguous, the courts will uphold it. The legacy of the farm is specific, because the property is named. It is not money to buy a farm, it is that particular farm. It is a basic rule that if the deceased disposed of an item making up a specific or special legacy, that legacy is adeemed and nothing is payable to the beneficiary in its place. The motives of the testator in disposing of the item are not relevant. Tough luck, Cuthbert!

(b) Conditional institute or substitute?

The technical name for a "whom failing" provision is a destination-over. If, as in this case, the institute (Bill) survives the testator, he takes a full vested right and the property, both heritable and moveable, is his to dispose of as he wishes. Thus, he could sell any or all of it, give it away or dispose of it by will. If, as is possible in this case, he does none of these things, Freda may have at least some cause for optimism. Augustus' will may have provided its own rules, but if not, certain presumptions will come into play. If Freda was a conditional institute, any rights of succession to the property will have flown off when Bill inherited. If, on the other hand, Freda was a substitute she could still inherit, provided—and always provided—that Bill has not already alienated the property. The presumption is that if the property is heritable, the alternative legatee is a substitute, but if it is moveable, the legatee is a conditional institute. Applying these principles, Freda could inherit the house but not the shares. Good cases in point are *Crumpton's J.F. v Barnardo's Homes* (1917) and *Watson v Giffen* (1884) in Chapter 7.

APPENDIX 2: A TYPICAL TRUST DISPOSITION AND SETTLEMENT

The undernoted trust disposition and settlement might be considered fairly typical. The style of the document indicates that it has been drawn up in a traditional manner, perhaps some years ago. It does not, for example, contain the now common provision of postponing vesting for a period of 30 days after the testator's death. Space does not permit comment on every item, but attention is drawn to particular points by the comments in italics. The testing clause and signatures have been omitted.

TRUST DISPOSITION AND SETTLEMENT OF JAMES BROWN

I, JAMES BROWN, Chartered Architect, Eleven Low Causeway, Inverdrearie, for the settlement of my means and estate after my death, do hereby ASSIGN, DISPONE and CONVEY to and in favour of my brother, NIGEL BROWN, Seventeen Anniesland Cross, Glasgow, my sister Mrs MAVIS BROWN or BYRD, Twenty Jute Street, Dundee and ALEXANDER FAIRSERVICE WYSE, Solicitor in Inverdrearie and to the acceptors and acceptor, survivors and survivor of them as trustees and trustee for the purposes aftermentioned (the trustees or trustee for the time being acting hereunder being hereinafter referred to as "my trustees") the whole means and estate, heritable and moveable, real and personal, wheresoever situated, which may belong to me or over which I shall have power of disposal at my death; And I appoint my trustees to be my executors; But these presents are granted in trust always for the following purposes: *[Yes, a bit verbose and slightly pompous, but reasonably clear. The testator is clearly setting up a trust which overlaps, but continues beyond, the period of executry. He prudently nominates a plurality of trustees; one might decline, another might predecease. The trustees are also expressly appointed as executors; this is common but not essential since testamentary trustees are statutorily executors, unless others are specifically appointed in the will.]*

FIRST For payment of my debts and funeral expenses and the expenses of administering the trust hereby created. *[This clause is not a requirement, but it is traditional.]*

SECOND I direct my trustees to make over the following specific legacies: (A) to my neighbour, Jack Spratt, Thirteen Low Causeway, Inverdrearie, my grand piano; *[The rules on ademption of specific legacies are covered in Chapter 6.]* (B) to my devoted Secretary, Miss Judith Panting, Eight Drumlie Street, Inverdrearie, provided she be in my employment at the date of my death, my grandfather clock; *[A classic example of a suspensive condition or a condition precedent. If the beneficiary fails to fulfil the condition of being in the testator's service at the time of his death, she acquires no right and the clock is part of the residue.]* (C) to my old friend, Magnus Merryman, Twelve Hope Street, Aberdeen, whom failing to his wife, my gold hunter pocket watch. *[A clear example of a destination-over, with Magnus's wife being called as conditional institute; if both predecease the testator, the watch forms part of the residue.]*

THIRD I direct my trustees to pay, as soon as convenient after my death but without interest to the date of payment, the following general legacies: (A) to each of my nephews and nieces, Peter Brown, David Brown, Graeme Brown, Joan Brown and Cynthia Brown or Green who shall survive me, the sum of One Thousand Pounds; *[There will be no accretion if one or more of this class predeceases.]* (B) to the Kirk Session of the Martyrs' Church, Inverdrearie, the sum of Five Thousand Pounds to be applied towards the refurbishment of the Church steeple, declaring that a simple receipt signed by the Kirk Treasurer for the time being shall be sufficient discharge for my trustees. *[This provision could be somewhat dated. The Church may have changed its name or united with another; perhaps the steeple was demolished five years ago! Unfortunately, no dispositive discretion is given to the trustees in the event of failure and there is a possibility that such a restricted provision could fail. The stipulation for a simple receipt to be an adequate discharge is sensible.]*

FOURTH I cancel the debt of Two Thousand pounds owing to me by Caleb Whyte, Forty Alexandra Street, Inverdrearie so far as the same, both capital and interest, is outstanding and unpaid at the date of my death. *[A nice gesture on the testator's part. Such a provision counts as a general legacy, should the matter of abatement arise.]*

FIFTH In the event of my wife Mrs Margaret Black or Brown surviving me, I direct my trustees to pay to her during all the days of her life (but subject as hereinafter provided) the free annual income of the residue of the trust estate, but that for her alimentary liferent use only *[Alimentary liferent is explained in Chapter 6.]* and declaring that out of the said income my wife shall be bound, to the satisfaction of my trustees, suitably to maintain and educate such of our children as remain in family with her and are unable reasonably to provide for themselves, as to which my trustees shall be the sole judges; *[The late Mr Brown might not have won awards for political correctness!]* with power to my trustees, should they consider the said income insufficient for the suitable maintenance and education as aforesaid of my wife and our children to encroach upon capital as they may consider necessary for the said purposes but so that such payments shall not exceed one third of the capital of the residue of my estate; *[There can only be encroachment on capital to provide income for the liferenter if, as in this case, express authority is given.]* declaring however that in the event of my said wife entering into a further marriage after my death, the foregoing liferent provision in her favour shall forthwith cease and determine and the said residue of my estate shall be dealt with as hereinafter provided; *[The testator is ensuring that the family wealth is not reduced by the widow taking anything into a subsequent marriage. He is seeking to make adequate provision for* *his widow without drastically reducing what will eventually come to his children.]* And I direct that the provisions of the Apportionment Act 1870 or of any other statute dealing with apportionment shall not apply to my estate. *[Mr Brown's solicitor would have put in this clause, disapplying the 1870 Act, to avoid the complicated calculations that would otherwise apply.]*

SIXTH In the event of my wife surviving me, then on her death or remarriage as hereinbefore provided, or, in the event of her predeceasing me, then on my death *[A classic example of fixing a certain day. If the wife dies before the testator, the liferent provision fails entirely. If she does survive, it is certain that the liferent will eventually end, either by her death or remarriage. This points to the fiars taking an immediate vested right on their father's death.]*, I direct my trustees to pay and make over the rest, residue and remainder of my means and estate equally among such of my children Alexander, Roderick and Samantha as shall be then in life, together with any children then in life who may be born to my said wife and myself after the making of this will *[This is stated not only for the sake of clarity but to ensure that there is no danger of a subsequently born child invoking the conditio si testator and thus pushing the entire estate into intestacy.]*, declaring that if any of my children shall predecease the date of division under this clause *[If his wife predeceases, the date of division is the testator's death. If his wife survives, the date of division is the end of the liferent. Children, in any event, take an immediate vested right on their father's death.]*, leaving issue who shall survive the said date, such issue shall come in place of their parent and take *per stirpes* if more than one, the share original and accresced, which his, her or their parent would have taken if then alive. *[Any child who survives the testator takes a vested right at the date of his death; similarly the issue of any of Mr Brown's children who survive his death but die before the date of division inherit that vested right. However, if a child survives the testator, but dies before the date of division leaving no issue, that child's share would be subject to defeasance and would accresce to the shares applicable to the other children.]*

SEVENTH I provide and declare that in addition to the powers, privileges and immunities of gratuitous trustees by statute and under common law, my trustees shall have the fullest powers of and in regard to retention, realisation, investment, administration, management and division of my estate as if they were absolute beneficial owners thereof *[This would have been inserted to ensure that the trustees would not have to observe the somewhat irksome investment provisions of the Trustee Investment Act 1961, now abolished, so the provision is now redundant.]* with power to my trustees to appoint any one or more of their own number or any other person to act as factor or solicitor to the trust hereby created and to allow him, her or them the same professional remuneration in respect of such actings to which he, she or they would have been entitled if not a trustee or trustees; *[Mr Wyse, the solicitor, would have ensured that this part of the clause was included—otherwise, as a gratuitous trustee, he would be unable to make any charge for his professional services.]* And I revoke all prior testamentary writings executed by me. *[Hopefully, any prior will has also been physically destroyed, either by the testator or by his solicitor, after express instructions.]* IN WITNESS WHEREOF. . .

INDEX

Abatement
  practical example, 45
  rules, on, 45
Accumulation of income
  see also **Void conditions**
  legal rights, 43
  meaning, 43
  rules, on, 43
  statutory provisions, 42, 43
Accretion
  see also **Legacies**
  legal presumptions, 60, 61
  illustration, of, 61
  joint and several legacies, 60
  meaning, 60
  severance, and, 60, 61
Ademption
  special legacies, 46
Annuities
  duration, 46
  inflation, 47
  inter vivos, 46
  liferent, distinguished, 47
    and see **Liferent**
  mortis causa, 46, 47
  payment method, 47
  periodical fixed payment, 46
  termination, 46
  trustees, and, 47
    and see **Trustees**
Ante-nuptial marriage contract trusts
  operation, of, 73
Approbate and reprobate
  legal rights, and, 16
    and see **Legal rights**
  meaning, of, 16

Beneficiary
  children, 77, 78
  heirs, 77
  identification, of, 75–78, 106
  issue, 78

Beneficiary—*cont.*
  next-of-kin, 77
  payment, to, 106
  powers, of, 107
  rights, of, 95
  spouses, 78
Bond of caution
  requirement, for, 29, 83

Charities
  legal status, 103
  public register, 98
  Scottish Charity Regulator (OSCR), 98, 99
  statutory provisions, 98
Children
  adopted children, 13, 78
  definition, 77
  illegitimate children, 78, 106
  legal rights, 13, 16, 17
    and see **Legal rights**
Civil partnerships
  inheritance tax, 82
  legal rights, 12 16, 17, 21
  prior rights, 18
  relict's part, 12
  rights, 26
  same sex partnerships, 1
  special destination, and, 69
    and see **Special destination**
  statutory provisions, 1
  surviving partners, 1
Codicil
  example, 63
  form, of, 63
  function, 63
  purpose, 63
Cohabitation
  cohabitees
    definition, 27
    entitlement, 27
    legal rights, 12
    relationship, between, 27

Cohabitation—*cont.*
cohabitees—*cont.*
relict's part, 12
rights, 27
intestacy, and, 27
special destination, and, 68, 69
and see **Special destination**
statutory provisions, 1, 27
Collateral Line
meaning, 14
Collation *inter liberos*
examples, 15
meaning, 15
Common calamity
examples, 9, 10
legal presumptions, 9–11
multiple deaths, 10, 11
simultaneous death, 9
special destination, and, 72
and see **Special destination**
succession rights, 9, 10
Company shares
income, from, 48
valuation, 87, 88
Conditio si testator
common law presumption, 58
conditio si institutus, distinguished, 57
operation, of, 58, 66
Corporeal property
nature, of, 3

Dead's part
intestacy, and, 22–24
meaning, 22
order of distribution, 22, 23
order of succession, 22
representation, and, 23
Death
cremation, 80, 81
death certificate, 79
information requirements, 79
insurance policies, 8
and see **Insurance policies**
legal presumptions, 7, 8
medical certificate, 79
organ donation, 80
overseas, 80, 81
place, 7
procedures, following, 79
proof, 8
registration, 79, 80

Death—*cont.*
simultaneous deaths, 9
see also **Common calamity**
time, 7
Debts
incidence of debts
creditors' rights, 93
funeral expenses, 91, 92
heritable debts, 93
inheritance tax, 92
insurance policies, 93
legal rights, 93
mortgage debts, 93, 94
moveable debts, 93
preferred debts, 92
prior rights, 93
secured debts, 92
testamentary provisions, 94
payment of debts
insufficient funds, 92
liability, 91, 92
order of payment, 91, 92
pari passu, 91, 92
privileged debts, 91
unsecured creditors, 91
valid claims, 91
Destination-over
heritable property, 52, 53
and see **Heritable property**
legal presumptions, 53
legatees
conditional institute, 52, 53
institute, 52, 53
substitute, 52, 53
testator's intentions, 52, 53
moveable property, 52, 53
and see **Moveable property**
vesting, and, 56
and see **Vesting**
'whom failing' provision, 52
Donations *mortis causa*
legal presumptions, 73, 74
proof, 74
status, of, 73
Dwellinghouse right
entitlement, 19
joint property, 19
multiple properties, 20
special destination, 19, 20
and see **Special destination**
statutory provisions, 19
value of benefit, 19

'Eik'
application, for, 84
grant, of, 84
Examination questions/answers
general comments, 108–109
sample questions, 109–116
Executors
appointment, 28, 81
bond of caution, 29
confirmation
additional confirmation, 84
ad non executa, 84
application, 83
bond of caution, 83
corrective inventory, 84
foreign property, 84
need, for, 82, 90
procedure, 81, 82
will, lodging of, 83
debts
see **Debts**
discharge, of, 96
duties, 82, 83, 90–91, 97
'eik' grant of, 84
executor-dative, 28, 29
executor-nominate, 28, 29, 81
function, 28
ingathering of property, 83
intestacy, and, 28
intromit with estate
confirmation requirement, 81, 82
inheritance tax, 82
right, to, 28, 29
inventory of estate
see **Inventory of estate**
oath, taken by, 89
rearrangements after death
deed of family arrangement, 95,
96
election to vary, 96
specific assets, 95
tax advantages, 95, 96
small estates procedure, 89–90
trust disposition and settlement, 83
and see **Trust disposition and
settlement**
trustees, as, 81, 83, 97

Fixtures
heritable property, 4
moveable property, 4
Furniture right
entitlement, 20

Furniture right—*cont.*
multiple properties, 20
scope, 20
statutory provisions, 20
value of benefit, 20

Gender
non-discrimination, 5
Goodwill
business goodwill, 3

Heir
unworthy, 94–95
Heritable property
destination-over, 52, 53
and see **Destination-over**
fixtures, 4
heritage, 3
joint title, 85
liferent, and, 3, 48
and see **Liferent**
mortgaged property, 4
moveable property, distinguished, 2,
3, 93
passing, 3
sasine title, 85
secured loans, 4
Historical background
biblical origins, 2
feudal origins, 3
survivors' rights, 2

Incorporeal property
nature, of, 3
Inheritance tax (IHT)
civil partners, 82
exemptions, 82
Form(IHT 200), 82
liability, 7
spouses, 82
statutory provisions, 6
threshold, 82
transfers of property, 82
valuation, 6
Insurance policies
death, and, 8
inheritance tax, 72
proceeds, 72
statutory provisions, 72
vested rights, 72
Intestate succession
cohabitation, and, 26, 27
and see **Cohabitation**

Intestate succession—*cont.*
  division of estate
    dead's part, 18
    examples, 24–26
    legal rights, 18
    order, of, 22, 23
    prior rights, 18
  executors, and, 28
    and see **Executors**
  meaning, 17
  partial intestacy, 18, 21, 94
  prior rights, 18
    and see **Prior rights**
  rules, 18, 29, 30
Inventory of estate
  see also **Executors**
  bank/building society accounts, 87
  cash in house, 86
  company shares, 87
  confirmatory purposes, 82, 83
  corrective inventory, 84
  drafting, 84, 85
  Form (C1), 82, 86
  heritable property
    description, 85
    joint title, 85
    mortgaged property, 86
    value, 86
    and see **Heritable property**
  household furniture, 86
  income tax repayment, 88
  inheritance tax liability, 82
  listing of property, 85
  lodging, of, 83
  misdescription, 83
  motor car, 87
  moveable debts, 89
  national savings, 87
  overvaluation, 84
  personal effects, 86
  purpose, 82
  securities, 88
  uncashed dividend warrants, 89
  undervalue, 83
  unit trusts/ISAs/PEPs, 88

Judicial factors (JFs)
  appointment, 105
  authority, 106
  function, 105, 106

Legacies
  abatement, and, 45

Legacies—*cont.*
  accretion
    see **Accretion**
  ademption, 46
  cumulative, 62
  legatum rei alienae, 46
  numbering, 61
  substitutional, 62
  types
    general legacies, 44, 45
    residual legacies, 44, 45
    special legacies, 44, 45
  vesting
    see **Vesting**
Legal rights
  approbate and reprobate, 16
  children, 13, 16, 17
  civil partners, 12, 16, 17, 21
  cohabitation, 12
    and see **Cohabitation**
  final settlement, 17
  fixed at death, 11
  intestate succession, 5, 11, 17
    and see **Intestate succession**
  legitim, 12, 13
    and see **Legitim**
  limitation period, 17
  nature, of, 11
  net moveable estate, 11, 21
  origins, 11
  prior rights, 11
    and see **Prior rights**
  relict's part, 12
    and see **Relict's part**
  spouses, 12, 16, 17, 21
  testamentary provisions, 17
    and see **Testamentary provisions**
  testate succession, 5, 11
    and see **Testate succession**
Legitim
  adopted children, 13
  collation *inter liberos*, 15
  fund
    calculation, 17
    division, of, 14
    nature, of, 17
  renunciation, 15, 16
  representation concept, 13
  step-children, 14
  surviving children, 13
Liferent
  alimentary, 49, 50
  annuities, distinguished, 47

Liferent—*cont.*
assignment, 50
company share income, 48
'courtesy', 3
entitlement, 47–49
heritable property, and, 48
inter vivos, 47
meaning, of, 3
mineral rights, 47, 48
mortis causa, 47
occupancy right, distinguished, 50
ownership, and, 48
property rights, 47–49
remarriage, and, 48
right of fee, 47
'terce', 3
timber rights, 47
Living will
concept, of, 7

Motor cars
status, of, 20, 87
value, of, 87
Moveable property
destination-over, 52, 53
and see **Destination-over**
fixtures, 4
heritable property, distinguished, 2, 3, 93
and see **Heritable property**
partnership assets, 5

Net moveable estate
claims, 11, 21
meaning, 11
Next-of-kin
common law, at, 28
legacy, to, 77
Nominations
effect, of, 72
indemnity, 72
payments, 72
revocation, 72

Organ transplants
authorisation, 80
donor cards, 80
medical research, 80
statutory provisions, 1, 80

Partnerships
assets, 5

Partnerships—*cont.*
farming partnerships, 5
moveable property, 5
Prior rights
availability
children, 19
civil partners, 18
spouses, 18
claim, for, 18, 19
dead's part, 22
and see **Dead's part**
dwellinghouse right, 19
and see **Dwellinghouse right**
financial provision, 21
furniture right, 20
and see **Furniture right**
intestate succession, and, 18
and see **Intestate succession**

Relict's part
civil partners, 12
cohabitees, 12
common law spouse, 12
legal rights, 12
meaning, 12
Residue clause
example, of, 51
home-made wills, 51
purpose, 51
rules
abatement, 51
ademption, 51

Special destination
background, 67
civil partnerships, 69
cohabitees, 68, 69
common calamity, and, 72
effect, of, 19, 20, 70
evacuation, 69, 70
heritable property, 67, 68
incorporeal moveable property, 71
joint title, 86
later wills, effect of, 69
meaning, 67
survivorship destination, 70
use, of, 68, 69
Survivorship
exceptions, 56
legal presumptions, 9, 10
legal rights, 56, 57
and see **Legal rights**

Survivorship—*cont.*
proof requirements, 9, 10
simultaneous deaths, 9
see also **Common calamity**
survivors' rights, 9

Testamentary provisions
annuities
see **Annuities**
destination-over
see **Destination-over**
legacies
see **Legacies**
legal presumptions, 40
liferent
see **Liferent**
professional advice, on, 50
residue clause
see **Residue clause**
void conditions, 40–44
and see **Void conditions**
Testate succession
see also **Wills**
advantage, 30
disposal of property, 30
Testator
capacity to test
circumvention, 31
facility, 31
undue influence, 31, 32
intestate succession, 5
and see **Intestate succession**
legacies, 5
see also **Legacies; Testamentary provisions**
rights, 5
sanity, 31
testate succession, 5
and see **Testate succession**
Trust disposition and settlement
effect, 97
example, 116–120
executors, and, 83
Trustee(s)
administration of estate, 100
annuities, and, 47
and see **Annuities**
appointment, of, 100, 104
assumption, 104
breach of trust, 104
charity trustee, 100
company share certificates, and, 83
conflict of interests, 101

Trustee(s)—*cont.*
definition, 100
discharge, of, 107–108
distribution of estate, 100
due care, 100
duties, 100–102
executors, as, 81, 83, 97
indemnity clause, 104
insufficient assets, 103, 104
investment, and, 1, 102
judicial factors (JFs)
see **Judicial factors (JFs)**
liability, of, 103, 104, 107
payment, 101, 102
personal attention, 101
powers, 1, 102, 103
removal, 105
resignation, 105
responsibilities, 100
title to property, 97, 99, 100
Trusts
common law, 96
constitution, 97
creation, of, 97
inter vivos, 96
mortis causa, 96
private trusts
beneficiaries, 97, 107
tax liability, 98
variation, 98
public trust
charitable trusts, 98
cy-près scheme, 99
legal status, 103
purpose, 98
rearrangement/reorganisation, 99
purpose, restrictions on, 105
statutory provisions, 96
termination, 106, 107
trust disposition and settlement, 97
use, of, 96

Unworthy heir
forfeiture, by, 94, 95

Vesting
see also **Legacies**
age attainment, 55
concept, of, 53
date of vesting
certain day, 55
uncertain day, 54, 55, 56
defeasance, 56

Vesting—*cont.*
destination-over, and, 56
examples, 58–60
postponement, 54
security, involved in, 55
survivorship rule
conditio si institutus, 57
exceptions, to, 56
legal rights, 56, 57
suspensive condition, 55
vested rights, 53, 54, 56
Void conditions
accumulation of income, 42, 43
illegality, 40
immorality, 40
impossibility, 40
liferents, and, 44
and see **Liferents**
objectionable conditions, 41, 42
pro non scripto, 41
public policy, and, 40
repugnancy, 42

Will substitutes
nominations
see **Nominations**
special destination
see **Special destination**
Wills
see also **Will substitutes**
alterations and amendments
amendments, 62
codicils, 63
new provisions, 62, 63
professional practice, 66, 67
revocation, 64–66
beneficiary
see **Beneficiary**
capacity
minimum age, 78
testator, 31, 32
codicil, 63
and see **Codicil**
draft wills, 37
essential validity
capacity to test, 31, 32
form of words, 30, 31
home-made wills, 31
undue influence, 31, 32

Wills—*cont.*
examples, 38–40
existence, of, 29
formal validity
informality of execution, 33
notarial execution, 33, 34
post-1995 practice, 35
pre-1995 practice, 32, 33
probative form, 33
self-proving wills, 36
signatures, 36
undated documents, 35
vicarious subscription, 36
written will, 32, 35
granters
reading-over, 37
subscription, by, 35
holograph will
meaning, 34
validity, 34
intention to test, 37
interpretation
applicable law, 78
dispositive discretion, 76, 77
extrinsic evidence, 74–76
general rule, 74
precatory bequests, 77
testator's wishes, 74, 78
mutual wills, 67
probative form
adopted wills, 34, 35
attested will, 33, 34
holograph will, 34
self-proving wills, 36
registration, 81
revocation
earlier will destroyed, 64, 65
express declaration, 65
implication, by, 65
legal presumptions, 64, 66
methods, 64, 65
partial, 65
second will, loss of, 66
testamentary provisions
see **Testamentary provisions**
trust disposition and settlement, 30
and see **Trust disposition and settlement**